NEW JERSEY TRAVEL GUIDE 2025-2026

Audria M. Cha

Copyright © 2024 by Audria M. Cha

All rights reserved.

No part of this publication may be reproduced,
distributed, or transmitted in any form or by any means, including
photocopying, recording, or other electronic or mechanical methods,
without the prior written permission of the publisher.

Disclaimer:

This book is intended for informational purposes only. While every effort has been made to ensure accuracy, the author and publisher do not assume responsibility for any errors, omissions, or outcomes resulting from the use of this information. Readers are encouraged to verify details independently, including but not limited to prices, opening hours, and travel regulations, as they may change over time.

Trademarks & Copyrights:

All product names, logos, brands, and trademarks mentioned in this book are the property of their respective owners. The mention of any specific companies, business or attractions does not imply endorsement or affiliation.

New jersey travel guide 2025

New jersey travel guide 2025

CONTENTS

INTRODUCTION **6**
    Overview of New Jersey 8
    Why Visit New Jersey? 10

PLANNING YOUR TRIP **13**
    Best Time to Visit 13
    Visa & Travel Requirements 15
    How to Get to New Jersey: Transportation Options (Air, Train, Bus, Car) 18
    Currency and Tipping Culture 21

GETTING AROUND NEW JERSEY **25**
    Public Transportation: Trains, Buses, and Ferries 25
    Renting a Car: Tips and Best Practices 28
    Ride-Sharing Apps (Uber, Lyft) and Taxis 31

WHERE TO STAY **34**
    Best Areas to Stay in New Jersey 34
    Hotels, Resorts, and Vacation Rentals 37
    Budget Accommodation Options 40
    Unique Stays: Bed & Breakfasts and Historical Inns 44

TOP TOURIST ATTRACTIONS **47**
    The Jersey Shore: Beaches and Boardwalks 47
    Liberty State Park: Views of the Statue of Liberty 48
    Princeton University & Princeton's Historic District 49
    Atlantic City: Casinos, Boardwalk, and Nightlife 50
    The Delaware Water Gap National Recreation Area 51
    The Thomas Edison National Historical Park 52
    Adventure Aquarium in Camden 53

DINING IN NEW JERSEY **54**
    Must-Try New Jersey Foods: Pork Roll, Salt Water Taffy, and More 54
    Best Restaurants for Every Budget 55
    Food Festivals & Events 57
    Vegan and Vegetarian-Friendly Options 58

SHOPPING IN NEW JERSEY **59**
    Top Shopping Malls and Outlets in New Jersey 59
    Antique and Flea Markets in New Jersey 61
    Local Souvenirs and Crafts in New Jersey 62

OUTDOOR ADVENTURES **63**
    Hiking and Nature Trails in New Jersey 63
    Beaches and Water Sports in New Jersey 64
    Amusement Parks: Six Flags Great Adventure 65
    Ski Resorts and Winter Sports in New Jersey 65

NIGHTLIFE AND ENTERTAINMENT..67
Best Bars and Pubs in New Jersey.. 67
Live Music Venues and Clubs..68
Atlantic City: Casinos and Shows.. 69

CULTURAL ATTRACTIONS...70
Museums to Visit in New Jersey... 70
Performing Arts: Theatres and Music Venues.. 71
Historic Landmarks and Districts in New Jersey...72

DAY TRIPS FROM NEW JERSEY..74
Exploring New York City (A Short Train Ride Away)... 74
Visiting Philadelphia, Pennsylvania... 75
The Pocono Mountains... 76

PRACTICAL TRAVEL TIPS...77
Safety and Health Tips for Visitors in New Jersey... 77
What to Pack for Your New Jersey Trip.. 79
Useful Phrases and Local Etiquette..82

USEFUL RESOURCES..85
Emergency Contacts & Services in New Jersey..86
Language & Translation Help in New Jersey... 87

FINAL TIPS FOR FIRST-TIME VISITORS..89
Local Customs and Etiquette in New Jersey.. 89
Best Photo Ops in New Jersey... 90

INTRODUCTION

New Jersey, often overshadowed by its famous neighbors, New York and Pennsylvania, offers travelers a unique blend of culture, history, and natural beauty that makes it stand out in its own right. While many might think of the state as just a stopover or a commuter hub, those who take the time to explore its hidden gems discover a landscape rich in diversity—from sandy beaches to sprawling forests, historic landmarks to cutting-edge cities.

One such unexpected treasure is the Garden State's reputation for having the most diverse collection of cherry blossom trees in the United States, found in Newark's Branch Brook Park. In spring, the park transforms into a sea of soft pink blooms, drawing photographers, nature enthusiasts, and locals alike. But cherry blossoms are just one of the many lesser-known wonders of this state, offering travelers a chance to experience authentic history, stunning landscapes, and local flavors that remain largely unexplored by the masses.

If you're considering New Jersey as a destination, you're in for more than you might expect. From the bustling shore towns of Asbury Park to the quiet charm of Cape May's Victorian streets, New Jersey has a diverse collection of places that cater to every type of traveler. Whether you're an outdoor adventurer, a history buff, or someone looking to experience modern culture in one of the state's growing cities, you'll find much to explore here.

In this guide, you'll discover not only the iconic spots, such as Atlantic City's famous boardwalks and casinos, but also the lesser-known gems like the pristine beaches of Long Beach Island and the historical sites of Trenton, where pivotal moments in American history unfolded. For those interested in culture, New Jersey is a true melting pot. It's home to thriving arts districts, music festivals, and a food scene influenced by the many communities that have made the state their home. You'll also learn about New Jersey's stunning parks, the perfect backdrop for hiking, birdwatching, and kayaking, offering tranquil getaways from the busy cities.

But what truly sets New Jersey apart is its dual nature. It's a place where one can walk along the shore, visit art museums, and drive through scenic forests all in the same day. As a travel expert, my advice to you is to approach New Jersey with curiosity—it's a destination with more to offer than its reputation might suggest. You'll leave with a deeper understanding of a state that has long flown under the radar but is more than deserving of your attention. In this guide, I'll provide you with the essential insights to get the most out of your visit, helping you navigate the state's highlights and hidden treasures.

By the end of this guide, you'll not only understand why New Jersey is worth visiting, but you'll also know how to make the most of your time there. Whether you're looking to embrace the shore life, dive into history, or explore nature, New Jersey's distinct blend of culture, history, and natural beauty will leave you with lasting memories.

Overview of New Jersey

New Jersey, the Garden State, may be one of the smallest U.S. states by area, but it is one of the most densely populated, packed with a diverse range of attractions, rich history, and cultural significance. Located in the northeastern part of the country, New Jersey borders New York to the north and east, Pennsylvania to the west, and Delaware to the south. Its strategic position between two major metropolitan areas—New York City and Philadelphia—gives it a unique character as a hub of commerce, industry, and culture.

Geography and Landscape
Despite its size, New Jersey offers a surprisingly varied landscape. To the east, it boasts miles of coastline along the Atlantic Ocean, with popular beach towns like Atlantic City, Wildwood, and Cape May offering sun, sand, and iconic boardwalks. The western part of the state is more rural and mountainous, with the Delaware Water Gap National Recreation Area providing numerous opportunities for hiking, canoeing, and camping. Between these extremes, you'll find fertile farmland, dense forests, and scenic rivers that carve through the state's interior, making it an outdoor enthusiast's haven.

Economy and Industry
New Jersey's economy is one of the most robust in the nation, driven by a variety of sectors. It is a major player in pharmaceuticals, technology, finance, and telecommunications. Companies like Johnson & Johnson, Merck, and Prudential are headquartered in the state, alongside a growing number of tech startups in cities like Jersey City and Newark. The state is also a major transportation hub, with access to major ports and railways connecting it to global trade routes. Its proximity to New York and Philadelphia makes it an ideal location for businesses seeking access to these larger markets, while still offering a lower cost of living compared to those cities.

History and Culture
New Jersey has a rich historical legacy, particularly as one of the original 13 colonies. It played a critical role in the American Revolution, with important battles like the Battle of Trenton taking place here. Today, visitors can explore sites like the Princeton Battlefield and the Thomas Edison National Historical Park, where Edison invented the phonograph and the light bulb. The state's diverse cultural makeup is reflected in its many communities, with significant Italian, Irish, African American, and Latin American populations, each contributing to the state's vibrant arts, music, and food scenes.

Education and Innovation
New Jersey is home to some of the country's top educational institutions, including Princeton University, Rutgers University, and Stevens Institute of Technology. These institutions contribute to the state's reputation for innovation, particularly in research and technology. As a result, New Jersey has earned a place in the forefront of biotech, pharmaceuticals, and other high-tech industries. The state's commitment to education and innovation is one of the driving forces behind its strong economy and its thriving business landscape.

Transportation

With its proximity to both New York and Philadelphia, New Jersey is well-connected through a vast transportation network. The state boasts a comprehensive public transportation system, including NJ Transit trains and buses, which make commuting to and from New York City and other areas convenient. The Garden State Parkway, New Jersey Turnpike, and several interstate highways also provide easy access to neighboring states and beyond. Newark Liberty International Airport is one of the busiest airports in the U.S., offering both domestic and international flights.

Tourism and Recreation

Tourism is a significant part of New Jersey's economy. Visitors flock to the state for its beaches, boardwalks, amusement parks, and historical landmarks. The state also attracts those seeking nature, with more than 50 state parks offering hiking, camping, and outdoor activities. Additionally, New Jersey's cultural offerings, from its rich arts scene to its world-class dining, make it a great destination for tourists interested in the arts, food, and entertainment.

A Place for All

Whether you're looking for a beach getaway, a trip through history, or a taste of urban life, New Jersey offers something for everyone. It combines the energy of its cities with the charm of its small towns and natural beauty, creating a dynamic and diverse environment that continues to attract new residents, businesses, and visitors year-round.

Why Visit New Jersey?

New Jersey often flies under the radar when it comes to U.S. travel destinations, but don't let its understated reputation fool you—it's a state full of surprises. As one of the original 13 colonies, New Jersey has played a significant role in shaping the nation's history, and that legacy is still present today in its diverse cultural offerings, scenic beauty, and dynamic cities. It may not have the sprawling wilderness of the western states or the towering skyscrapers of New York, but what it does offer is unique, accessible, and often overlooked.

A Historic Backbone

For history enthusiasts, New Jersey is a goldmine of historical landmarks and heritage sites. One standout fact is that the state is home to more Revolutionary War battle sites than any other state, including famous locations like Princeton Battlefield and Monmouth Battlefield. The state's history goes beyond the American Revolution as well; Trenton, the state capital, was the site of significant moments in the Civil War and industrial revolution, and the Thomas Edison Center in Menlo Park celebrates the inventor's pivotal role in modern history. History buffs will find themselves stepping back in time, gaining insight into the origins of the nation while exploring well-preserved sites and engaging with local museums.

The Great Outdoors
Despite being one of the smallest states, New Jersey boasts an impressive variety of landscapes, from coastal shores to dense woodlands. The Delaware Water Gap, located along the border with Pennsylvania, is a prime example of the state's natural beauty, offering over 70,000 acres of protected land perfect for hiking, camping, and kayaking. For those seeking the thrill of the outdoors, the state also has miles of trails in the Appalachian Mountains, along with scenic lakes, rivers, and beaches. It's a state that offers nature lovers a chance to explore everything from rugged mountain landscapes to serene coastal views, all within a short drive from major cities.

Beach Resorts and Hidden Shore Towns
While many people associate New Jersey with its well-known shore towns like Atlantic City and Wildwood, there are quieter, lesser-known coastal spots that are just as appealing. Long Beach Island, with its charming small-town feel, pristine beaches, and friendly atmosphere, provides the perfect escape for those seeking a more relaxing and less crowded experience. For those who love history and charm, Cape May, with its Victorian architecture and vibrant seaside culture, offers a nostalgic trip back in time. These small, picturesque towns contrast nicely with the high-energy destinations like Atlantic City, offering a balance for all types of beachgoers.

Culinary Diversity
New Jersey is an unassuming powerhouse when it comes to food. Known for its diner culture and its place as the birthplace of the sub sandwich, New Jersey offers a rich, eclectic food scene that reflects its cultural diversity. If you find yourself in Hoboken, you can trace the city's Italian heritage through its abundance of Italian eateries. Meanwhile, the state's proximity to Philadelphia means you can't miss a proper Philly cheesesteak—served hot and fresh in Trenton or Camden. The local culinary scene spans from ethnic enclaves in places like Edison and Jersey City, where Indian, Middle Eastern, and Asian influences abound, to classic comfort foods like boardwalk fries and fresh seafood from the shore.

The Best of Both Worlds
Another reason to visit New Jersey is its proximity to major metropolitan areas. The state acts as a bridge between Philadelphia and New York City, making it an excellent base for travelers who want to explore both cities while staying outside the high cost and hustle of their urban centers. Jersey City offers stunning views of the Manhattan skyline and is home to a growing arts scene, while places like Princeton and Morristown provide a more laid-back atmosphere with cultural and educational institutions that rival the big cities. New Jersey's strategic location allows you to experience the best of both worlds: the high energy of major cities and the charm of small-town Americana.

A State of Innovation
New Jersey has always been a hub of innovation. Beyond its historical contributions, the state has a long history of technological advancements and innovation, particularly in the pharmaceutical, technology, and financial sectors. It's the birthplace of the modern radio and the assembly line (thanks to Thomas Edison's work in Menlo Park), and more recently, it's home to Silicon Alley, a growing tech and startup scene.

Those interested in technology, science, and industry will find plenty to explore, from research facilities to cutting-edge companies and industrial landmarks.

Festivals and Entertainment
New Jersey is not short on things to do year-round. Festivals, concerts, and sporting events make the state a lively destination no matter the time of year. From the North to Shore Music Festival, which spans multiple cities with a mix of music, film, and food, to the New Jersey Film Festival in New Brunswick, the state celebrates its local culture while drawing in global talent. In the fall, the state hosts agricultural fairs and pumpkin festivals that showcase New Jersey's agricultural heritage. Whether you're into music, arts, sports, or culinary delights, there's always something happening that reflects the diverse tastes and passions of the state's residents.

A Real-World Escape
For those looking for a destination that offers both cultural immersion and an authentic sense of place, New Jersey delivers on both fronts. Whether you're strolling through the scenic streets of Hoboken, exploring the natural beauty of its parks and forests, or indulging in its dynamic food scene, New Jersey offers an authentic and unique perspective on American life. It's a state that often surprises visitors—offering more than they might expect and leaving them with memories of its hidden charms, rich culture, and diverse landscapes.

If you're looking for a place that offers a mix of history, outdoor adventure, beach relaxation, cultural diversity, and culinary delights—all without the overwhelming crowds of bigger cities—New Jersey should be on your radar. A visit to this state reveals the beauty of its contrasts, where urban energy meets quiet retreats, and cultural richness intertwines with outdoor fun. New Jersey may not always be the first destination that comes to mind, but once you've been, it's easy to see why it's a state worth experiencing for yourself.

PLANNING YOUR TRIP

Best Time to Visit

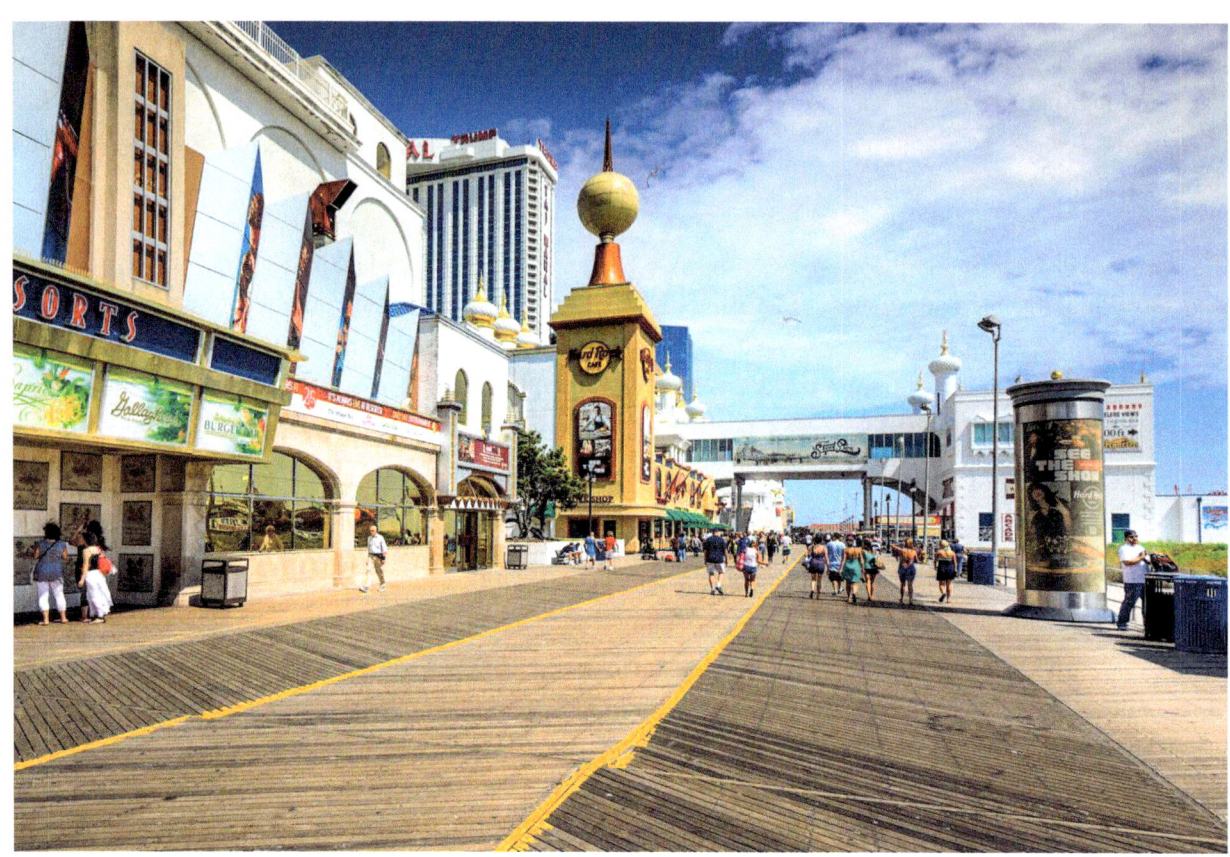

When considering the best time to visit New Jersey, the answer depends on the type of experience you're after. Whether you're aiming for a sunny beach day, a hike through autumn foliage, or attending a major event, New Jersey's diverse seasons provide plenty of options for travelers. Here's a breakdown of what to expect in each season to help you plan your visit.

Spring (March to May)
Spring is one of the most delightful times to visit New Jersey. The weather starts to warm up, and nature comes alive with colorful blooms, making it a great season for outdoor activities. Average temperatures range from the mid-40s to the low 70s, making it a comfortable time to explore the state's parks, gardens, and waterfronts. One of the standout events in spring is the annual cherry blossom festival at Branch Brook Park in Newark, which features the largest collection of cherry trees in the United States. If you're a fan of gardens and flowers, New Jersey's botanical gardens, such as the New Jersey Botanical Garden in Ringwood, come to life with a range of flowers in full bloom, offering excellent photo opportunities.

Summer (June to August)
If you're planning a beach vacation, summer is the prime time to visit New Jersey. The shore towns come alive with tourists and locals taking advantage of the state's long coastline. Beaches like Long Beach Island, Atlantic City, and Cape May attract visitors for their warm waters and vibrant beach culture. Summer temperatures can reach the 80s and occasionally into the 90s, with the humidity making it feel warmer, so be prepared for some heat. The summer season also brings a range of festivals and events, such as the Atlantic City Airshow and the North to Shore Music Festival. The lively atmosphere in coastal towns and the opportunity to explore the boardwalks make summer a great time for those looking for a quintessential beach experience. However, be mindful that it's also peak tourist season, so popular spots can get crowded.

Fall (September to November)
Autumn is perhaps the best time to experience New Jersey's natural beauty. The weather is cooler, with temperatures averaging between the low 60s and mid-70s, making it perfect for outdoor activities like hiking, biking, and scenic drives. The state's forests and parks, including the Delaware Water Gap and High Point State Park, burst into shades of red, orange, and gold, offering one of the most picturesque fall foliage displays in the region. For those who enjoy apple picking or pumpkin farms, fall is the perfect time to visit the rural towns in Sussex and Warren counties. Additionally, September through November is harvest season, and you'll find farmers' markets brimming with fresh produce, local cider, and baked goods. Fall also brings a quieter atmosphere to the shore towns, so if you prefer a more peaceful beach getaway, this is an ideal time to visit.

Winter (December to February)
Winter in New Jersey can be cold, with temperatures ranging from the mid-20s to low 40s, but it offers a different kind of charm. While the beaches are quieter and many of the tourist spots slow down, the holiday season brings a special atmosphere to the state. The cities and towns light up with festive decorations, and there are plenty of opportunities to visit holiday markets, enjoy ice skating, and take part in seasonal celebrations. For those who enjoy winter sports, New Jersey offers skiing and snowboarding at resorts like Mountain Creek and Campgaw Mountain, which are perfect for a weekend getaway. However, it's important to note that snow can be unpredictable in the state, so be prepared for potential weather delays if you're traveling during this season.

Off-Season (Mid-Week Visits and Non-Holiday Periods)
While the peak seasons of summer and holidays bring bustling crowds, visiting New Jersey during off-peak periods can be an enjoyable way to explore the state without the crowds. Traveling in midweek, especially during the shoulder seasons in late fall or early spring, allows you to enjoy many of New Jersey's top attractions with fewer tourists. Museums, parks, and historic sites are often less crowded, offering a more relaxed experience. Additionally, hotel prices tend to be lower during these times, making it a more affordable option for travelers on a budget.

Visa & Travel Requirements

When planning a trip to New Jersey, understanding visa and travel requirements is essential to ensure a smooth and hassle-free experience. Whether you're traveling from within the United States or internationally, there are specific guidelines you'll need to follow to enter the state. Below is a breakdown of key visa and travel requirements for visitors to New Jersey.

U.S. Visa Requirements for International Travelers
If you're coming from outside the United States, you will need to apply for a visa unless you're from a country that participates in the U.S. Visa Waiver Program (VWP). The most common types of visas for tourists are the B-1 (Business) and B-2 (Tourism) visas.

Visa Waiver Program (VWP)
Citizens of countries that are part of the VWP can travel to the U.S. without obtaining a visa for stays of 90 days or less. This program applies to visitors traveling for business or tourism purposes, and it includes over 39 countries such as the UK, France, Japan, and many European nations. However, travelers under the VWP must apply for an ESTA (Electronic System for Travel Authorization) prior to boarding a flight. This is an online application process that screens travelers for eligibility.

B-1/B-2 Tourist Visa

If you're not eligible for the VWP, you will need to apply for a B-2 visa. This visa is for tourists visiting the United States for leisure, including sightseeing, visiting family or friends, or attending events. The process involves completing the DS-160 form online, scheduling a visa interview at the U.S. embassy or consulate in your home country, and providing supporting documents such as proof of financial means, travel itinerary, and ties to your home country to ensure your return.

Key Documents Required for U.S. Visa Applications
Regardless of the type of visa, several documents are typically required:

Passport: Your passport must be valid for at least six months beyond your planned stay in the United States.

Visa Application Form (DS-160): Complete the DS-160 form online and upload your photo.

Visa Appointment Confirmation: After scheduling your visa interview, you will receive a confirmation that must be presented during the interview.

Visa Fee Receipt: The visa application fee varies depending on your nationality and the type of visa.

Supporting Documents: These may include financial documents, invitation letters, and proof of your travel plans.

U.S. Customs and Border Protection
Once you arrive in New Jersey, you'll be processed by U.S. Customs and Border Protection (CBP). At the port of entry, you'll need to provide your passport, visa (if applicable), and ESTA approval (for those traveling under the Visa Waiver Program). Be prepared to answer questions about your travel plans, accommodation, and the purpose of your visit. CBP will review your documents and may ask additional questions to ensure you comply with immigration laws.

Travel Insurance
Although travel insurance is not required for entry to the United States, it is highly recommended, especially for international travelers. A comprehensive travel insurance policy will cover medical emergencies, trip cancellations, lost luggage, and other unforeseen situations that can affect your journey. New Jersey has excellent healthcare facilities, but as a foreign visitor, you will need insurance to help cover any medical costs during your stay.

Transportation and Arrival in New Jersey
New Jersey is easily accessible by air, sea, and land. If you're arriving by air, the Newark Liberty International Airport (EWR) is the primary international gateway into the state, handling flights from around the world. Many international travelers also fly into John F. Kennedy International Airport (JFK) or LaGuardia Airport (LGA) in nearby New York City, which are well-connected to New Jersey by public transportation, including buses, trains, and taxis. After your flight, public transit options like NJ Transit

buses and trains can take you to various parts of the state, or you can choose a rental car for more flexibility.

Customs Declarations
When entering the United States, you will need to declare items you're bringing with you. This includes food, plants, animals, or other restricted items. Be prepared to fill out a CBP Declaration Form (usually provided during your flight). Failure to declare restricted items could lead to fines or confiscation of goods.

U.S. Customs Regulations for New Jersey
When entering the U.S., it's important to be aware of the customs regulations, which apply to travelers arriving in New Jersey as well. Some items, such as large amounts of currency, agricultural products, or certain electronics, may be subject to additional inspection or taxes. For a smooth experience, it's wise to familiarize yourself with what you can and cannot bring into the U.S. For example, fresh fruits and vegetables, plants, or meats are prohibited from being brought into the country, so be sure to check the guidelines before packing.

Departure and Reentry into the U.S.
If you're planning to leave and re-enter the U.S. during your visit to New Jersey, ensure that your visa or ESTA is valid for reentry. Some visa categories have restrictions on reentry, so be sure to check with the U.S. embassy or consulate for your specific visa details.

How to Get to New Jersey: Transportation Options (Air, Train, Bus, Car)

New Jersey is easily accessible from all over the United States and around the world, thanks to its strategic location in the northeastern U.S. Whether you're arriving by air, train, bus, or car, there are multiple options to get you into the state. Here's a detailed look at each of the most common transportation methods to help you decide the best way to reach New Jersey based on your preferences, budget, and convenience.

By Air: Flying Into New Jersey
New Jersey is well-served by several major airports, offering both domestic and international flights. The most convenient airport for most visitors is Newark Liberty International Airport (EWR), which is located in Newark, just a short drive from New Jersey's major cities, including Jersey City, Hoboken, and even Manhattan. Newark Liberty is one of the oldest airports in the United States and serves as a hub for United Airlines, offering a wide range of flights to and from destinations around the world.

Key Facts About EWR:
Location: In Newark, NJ, about 15 miles from Manhattan.

Direct Flights: Newark offers direct flights to and from major cities in the U.S., Europe, Asia, and Latin America.

Access to Public Transit: The airport is well-connected to New Jersey and New York City via NJ Transit trains, Amtrak, and the AirTrain Newark monorail. You can easily reach popular destinations like Manhattan, Hoboken, and Princeton by taking a direct train or bus from the airport.

For travelers flying into New York City, John F. Kennedy International Airport (JFK) and LaGuardia Airport (LGA) are also excellent options. Both airports are about an hour's drive from New Jersey, depending on traffic, and are connected to New Jersey through a variety of transport options, including buses, taxis, and ride-sharing services like Uber and Lyft.

By Train: Amtrak and NJ Transit
New Jersey is well-connected to major cities via an extensive train network, making train travel a popular choice for visitors coming from nearby states or even across the country.

Amtrak: Amtrak is a convenient option for long-distance travelers, offering routes from cities like Washington, D.C., Boston, and Chicago. The Amtrak Northeast Corridor line runs through New Jersey with stops in cities like Newark, Trenton, and New Brunswick, connecting passengers to popular destinations on the East Coast. From Amtrak stations, travelers can easily access other parts of New Jersey via NJ Transit.

Key Amtrak Stations: Newark Penn Station, Trenton Transit Center, New Brunswick Station.

Travel Time: From Washington, D.C. to Newark is about 3.5 hours; from Boston to Newark, it's roughly 4.5 hours.

NJ Transit: For those coming from within New Jersey or from nearby cities like Philadelphia, NJ Transit offers frequent and affordable service between New Jersey and neighboring states. NJ Transit operates commuter trains that link New Jersey to Penn Station in Manhattan, and it also runs buses and light rail services across the state.

Popular Routes: From New York's Penn Station to Newark, Hoboken, and other major towns in New Jersey.

Convenience: NJ Transit provides direct access to popular attractions like the Jersey Shore, Princeton University, and historic sites in towns like Morristown.

By Bus: Affordable and Convenient
Taking a bus to New Jersey is an affordable option for travelers looking to save money while still reaching key destinations. Several bus companies operate routes between New Jersey and major cities like New York City, Philadelphia, and Washington, D.C.

New Jersey Transit Buses: NJ Transit operates a robust network of buses within New Jersey and to nearby cities. If you're traveling within the state or from surrounding areas like Pennsylvania, NJ Transit buses are reliable, clean, and relatively inexpensive. They serve a variety of routes, including those that connect Newark, Hoboken, and Jersey City with key transit hubs in New York.

Private Bus Services: For longer trips, private bus companies like Greyhound, Megabus, and BoltBus provide affordable routes from major cities. For example, buses run regularly between New York City and Atlantic City, with travel times as short as 2 hours. These buses typically offer amenities like Wi-Fi and comfortable seating, making them a good choice for budget-conscious travelers.

Travel Time: From New York to Trenton is about 1 hour; from Philadelphia to Atlantic City is roughly 1.5 hours.

By Car: Self-Driving and Renting a Car
If you prefer flexibility and want to explore New Jersey at your own pace, driving is a great option. The state is conveniently accessible via major highways, including Interstate 95, Interstate 78, and Interstate 80, making it easy to drive to from New York City, Philadelphia, and beyond.

Renting a Car:
If you're flying into New Jersey and don't want to rely on public transportation, renting a car is a straightforward option. Newark Liberty International Airport and other nearby airports offer car rental services from major agencies such as Enterprise, Hertz, and Avis. Renting a car provides you with the freedom to explore New Jersey's cities, parks, and scenic coastal areas at your own pace.

Travel Time: From New York City to Newark takes about 30 minutes; from Philadelphia to Trenton, it's around 45 minutes.

Driving Tips: New Jersey has some of the busiest highways in the country, so be prepared for traffic, especially around rush hour in areas near Newark or on the Garden State Parkway.

Parking can be challenging in major cities like Hoboken, Jersey City, and Princeton. Be sure to check for parking garages or street parking regulations before you drive into these areas.

Currency and Tipping Culture

When visiting New Jersey, it's essential to understand the local currency and tipping culture to ensure smooth interactions and avoid confusion. Here's what you need to know to navigate both aspects of your trip with ease.

Currency: U.S. Dollar (USD)
The official currency of New Jersey, as with the rest of the United States, is the U.S. dollar (USD). All transactions, whether for dining, shopping, or services, will be in U.S. dollars. It's important to familiarize yourself with both paper bills and coins, as the U.S. currency system can be a bit different from that of other countries.

Paper bills: U.S. paper money comes in denominations of $1, $5, $10, $20, $50, and $100. The bills are typically the same size and color, with different portraits of notable American figures such as George Washington ($1), Abraham Lincoln ($5), and Alexander Hamilton ($10).

Coins: Coins are in the following denominations: penny (1 cent), nickel (5 cents), dime (10 cents), quarter (25 cents), and half dollar (50 cents). Most transactions will involve pennies, nickels, dimes, and quarters, especially for smaller purchases.

ATMs are widely available, and credit and debit cards are accepted almost everywhere in New Jersey, including at restaurants, hotels, shops, and attractions. If you're not accustomed to the U.S. dollar, a currency converter app or website can help you track exchange rates, especially if you're coming from abroad.

Currency Exchange and Banking
If you're traveling from abroad and need to exchange your home currency for U.S. dollars, there are plenty of options available at airports, exchange bureaus, and local banks. Many international airports, including Newark Liberty International Airport (EWR), offer currency exchange services, though the exchange rates at airports may not be the best. For better rates, consider using a local exchange service or withdrawing cash directly from ATMs, which often offer competitive rates and are easy to access.

Many businesses in New Jersey, particularly those near tourist areas, will accept credit cards in foreign currencies, but it's always a good idea to carry some U.S. dollars for smaller establishments or tips.

Tipping Culture: Understanding Expectations
Tipping is an integral part of the service culture in New Jersey, and throughout the United States. While tips are not mandatory, they are expected for many services, and failure to tip can be seen as a sign of dissatisfaction. Here's a breakdown of what to expect and how much to tip for various services.

Restaurants
In New Jersey, it's customary to tip between 15% and 20% of the total bill before tax. Some restaurants may include a service charge for large parties (usually 18%-20%), but it's always a good idea to check the bill to avoid double-tipping. The amount you tip should depend on the quality of service you receive—20% is standard for excellent service, while 15% is acceptable for average service. For outstanding service, you may consider tipping more than 20%.

For example: If your meal costs $50, a 15% tip would be $7.50, and a 20% tip would be $10.

Bars
Bartenders in New Jersey generally expect tips of around $1 to $2 per drink or 15% to 20% of the total bar tab. If you're ordering cocktails or drinks with a higher price, it's polite to increase your tip accordingly. If the bartender goes above and beyond, such as creating a custom cocktail or serving you in a busy setting, consider leaving a larger tip.

For example: If you order a $15 cocktail, a tip of $2 to $3 would be appropriate.

Taxis and Ride-Sharing

When using taxis or ride-sharing services like Uber and Lyft, tipping is common. A typical tip is 10% to 15% of the fare, though it can be adjusted based on service quality. In some cases, Uber and Lyft passengers have the option to add a tip directly through the app, which makes it easy and hassle-free.

For example: For a $20 ride, a tip of $2 to $3 is typical.

Hotels
Housekeepers, bellhops, and concierge staff also expect tips for their services. It's customary to tip $1 to $2 per night for hotel housekeeping, especially if your room was cleaned thoroughly. If a bellhop assists with your luggage, a tip of $1 to $2 per bag is appropriate. Concierge staff who provide specialized services, such as securing reservations or arranging tours, typically expect tips of $5 to $10, depending on the complexity of the request.

For example: If a bellhop helps you with two bags, a $2 to $4 tip is reasonable.

<u>Other Service Providers</u>
Valets: A tip of $2 to $5 for valet service is typical, especially when they retrieve your car.

Tour Guides: If you're taking a guided tour, tipping the guide $5 to $10 per person is common, depending on the length and quality of the tour.

Hairdressers and Spa Staff: For personal services, such as haircuts, massages, and other treatments, a tip of 15% to 20% is standard.

Important Considerations
Service Charges: Some upscale restaurants and establishments may automatically include a service charge on the bill, typically for large groups. If this happens, tipping on top of the service charge is not necessary, but if the service was exceptional, an extra tip can be a nice gesture.

Cash Tips vs. Card Tips: While it's acceptable to leave tips on your credit card for many services, cash tips are often preferred by workers, especially in restaurants, as they get immediate access to the funds. If possible, carry cash for tipping, as it's appreciated more directly.

Tipping Etiquette: Why It Matters
Tipping is more than just a financial transaction—it's a way of showing appreciation for good service. In many cases, tips make up a significant portion of a service worker's income, particularly in industries like restaurants and hospitality. Understanding the tipping culture in New Jersey and adhering to expected practices is a way to support workers and contribute positively to the local economy.

While tipping is common in New Jersey, it's always important to remember that the amount should reflect the quality of service you receive. If you feel the service was poor, it's okay to tip less or leave a comment for the management to address the issue. Conversely, if you receive exceptional service, a larger tip can be a great way to show your appreciation.

GETTING AROUND NEW JERSEY

Public Transportation: Trains, Buses, and Ferries

Getting around New Jersey is easy thanks to its efficient and comprehensive public transportation system. Whether you're traveling from one city to another, heading to the beach, or navigating the suburban areas, public transit options such as trains, buses, and ferries offer convenience and affordability. Here's a guide to the key public transportation options in New Jersey to help you plan your trip.

Trains: Fast, Reliable, and Widely Accessible
New Jersey's train system is robust, with multiple options that connect the state to both nearby cities and destinations within the state. NJ Transit operates the majority of train services, providing a reliable and cost-effective way to travel between New Jersey's cities, suburbs, and neighboring states like New York and Pennsylvania.

Key Routes and Stations
Northeast Corridor Line: This line is one of the busiest in New Jersey, running from Trenton through major hubs like Newark Penn Station, Hoboken Terminal, and onto Manhattan's Penn Station. It's ideal

for those traveling into New York City, as the train ride takes about 20-30 minutes from Newark and around an hour from Trenton.

North Jersey Coast Line: This route connects Long Branch, Asbury Park, and other shore towns with Newark and New York City. It's perfect for visitors looking to enjoy New Jersey's coastal attractions while remaining connected to the larger metropolitan areas.

Raritan Valley Line: Linking High Bridge, Somerville, and Newark, this line is a great option for those heading into the central and western parts of the state.

NJ Transit trains are generally clean, efficient, and provide comfortable seating. Tickets can be purchased at kiosks or on the NJ Transit mobile app, which also offers real-time updates on train schedules and potential delays.

For those heading further into the state, Amtrak also operates long-distance trains, with several stops in New Jersey, including Trenton and Newark, connecting travelers to cities like Washington, D.C., and Boston.

Buses: Flexible and Extensive Network
Buses in New Jersey provide a great way to travel within the state and to nearby cities. NJ Transit runs an extensive network of buses, serving areas not covered by trains, including rural towns and smaller communities. Additionally, private companies like Greyhound and Megabus operate long-distance routes to and from New Jersey, making bus travel an affordable option for visitors.

Local Buses
NJ Transit Buses: These buses run across the state, connecting urban and suburban areas. Major routes include trips from Trenton to Philadelphia and from Newark to Jersey City, making them a practical option for daily commuting or casual sightseeing. Buses are often a good choice when traveling to areas that are not served by train, such as more remote regions in central and southern New Jersey.

Light Rail: In cities like Jersey City and Hoboken, light rail systems operated by NJ Transit are an excellent way to navigate the local urban areas. The Hudson-Bergen Light Rail connects residents and visitors to various attractions, including the waterfront and residential neighbourhoods.

Tickets for local bus routes can be purchased on board, at ticket vending machines, or via the NJ Transit mobile app. Buses are a great option for those exploring New Jersey's towns and cities, offering frequent stops and coverage across the state.

Long-Distance Buses
Greyhound and Megabus: If you're coming from a nearby city, long-distance buses can be a budget-friendly alternative to flying or driving. These services offer routes from Philadelphia, Washington, D.C., and New York City into major New Jersey hubs like Newark and Trenton. With spacious seating

and free Wi-Fi on some buses, these services provide comfort and affordability, often for less than the cost of train travel.

Ferries: Scenic and Relaxing
For a truly unique way to travel around New Jersey, consider taking a ferry. The state's proximity to the water offers a few ferry routes that not only provide transportation but also offer scenic views of the skyline, bridges, and coastline. Ferries are popular for those heading to New York City or traveling between waterfront destinations in New Jersey.

Key Ferry Routes
New Jersey to New York City: Ferries from Hoboken, Weehawken, and Jersey City provide a direct and scenic route to Manhattan. The NY Waterway ferry service operates several routes that depart from various locations in New Jersey and land at Manhattan's Pier 11/Wall Street, Midtown Manhattan, and Battery Park City. The views of the Manhattan skyline and the Statue of Liberty during the ride are exceptional, making it a memorable trip for both commuters and tourists.

Atlantic City to Brigantine Island: For a more local experience, the Atlantic City Ferry offers a direct route to Brigantine Island for those visiting the New Jersey Shore. The ferry operates seasonally and provides a relaxing, scenic route to the island's beaches and casinos.

Ferries are a fantastic option when traveling to or from the waterfront areas in New Jersey, and they offer a memorable view of the state's famous waterways. Tickets are available for purchase at ferry terminals or through apps like NY Waterway for online booking.

Travel Passes and Discounts
For visitors planning to use public transportation frequently, several options can save money. NJ Transit offers a 7-Day Pass for unlimited travel on trains, buses, and light rail, which is ideal for tourists staying for a week. If you're only using public transit for a few days, the One-Day Pass may also be an economical choice. Discounts are often available for seniors, people with disabilities, and children, so check the NJ Transit website for more details.

Renting a Car: Tips and Best Practices

Renting a car in New Jersey offers flexibility, allowing you to explore the state's diverse regions at your own pace. Whether you're visiting the bustling cities, scenic beaches, or historic towns, having your own vehicle can enhance your trip. However, to make the most of your car rental experience, there are a few tips and best practices to keep in mind.

1. Choosing the Right Rental Agency
There are numerous car rental agencies in New Jersey, with most located at major airports like Newark Liberty International Airport (EWR) or in key cities like Jersey City and Hoboken. Well-known agencies include Enterprise, Hertz, Avis, Budget, and National. If you're flying into New Jersey, consider renting a car directly from the airport for convenience. However, renting from an airport location may come with higher fees due to extra charges from the airport itself.

When choosing a rental agency, always compare rates and check for hidden fees. Many rental companies offer competitive prices, but it's essential to factor in taxes, insurance, and optional add-ons like GPS or car seats. Websites like Kayak, Expedia, and Rentalcars.com allow you to compare prices across different agencies for the best deals.

2. Understand Rental Policies
Before booking a rental, thoroughly read the agency's rental policies. There are often various rules and conditions you might overlook, which can affect your overall experience.

Age Restrictions: Most car rental agencies in New Jersey require drivers to be at least 21 years old, although drivers under 25 may be subject to an additional "young driver" surcharge. In some cases, this surcharge can be quite hefty, so it's important to check if it applies to your booking.

Driver's License: You'll need a valid driver's license to rent a car in New Jersey. For international visitors, an International Driver's Permit (IDP) is generally recommended, though some rental agencies may accept a foreign license without the IDP.

Fuel Policy: Rental agencies typically offer one of two fuel policies: full-to-full or full-to-empty. With the full-to-full policy, you return the car with a full tank of gas, and you're only charged for the fuel you used. With full-to-empty, you pay for a full tank upfront, but you don't get a refund for unused fuel. It's often more economical to choose the full-to-full option.

3. Insurance and Coverage
Car rental insurance is an essential part of the rental process, but understanding your options is key to saving money. While it's tempting to purchase the rental agency's insurance package, you may already be covered through your personal car insurance or credit card.

Personal Car Insurance: Many car insurance policies extend to rental cars, so check with your insurance provider before booking. If your personal policy covers rentals, you can decline the rental agency's insurance to avoid paying for duplicate coverage.

Credit Card Insurance: Some major credit cards (like those from Chase, American Express, and MasterCard) provide rental car insurance coverage if you use the card to pay for the rental. However, this coverage typically only applies to damage and theft, not liability, so read the terms carefully before declining the agency's coverage.

Collision Damage Waiver (CDW): This option protects you from paying for damages to the rental car in case of an accident. While it's often pricey, some travelers find it reassuring, especially when traveling in unfamiliar areas.

4. Inspect the Car Before Driving Off
Before you drive off the lot, carefully inspect the rental car for any existing damage. Take note of any scratches, dents, or other imperfections on the car's body and document them with the agency staff, so you're not held responsible for damages you didn't cause. Many rental agencies will provide you with a form to record any damage, or they may take pictures for their records. If any issues arise later, you'll have proof that they existed before you drove off.

5. Navigating New Jersey's Roads
New Jersey's roads are generally well-maintained, but they can be challenging for visitors unfamiliar with the area. Here are some driving tips specific to the state:

Tolls: New Jersey has numerous toll roads, particularly on highways like the Garden State Parkway and New Jersey Turnpike. Tolls can be paid in cash or electronically via E-ZPass. Many rental companies offer E-ZPass transponders, which make toll payments more convenient, but be aware of additional fees for using this service.

Parking: Parking in New Jersey, especially in urban areas like Jersey City, Hoboken, and Newark, can be challenging and expensive. Look for parking garages, as street parking can be limited or subject to time restrictions. Some rental agencies also offer valet services for an additional fee.

Speed Limits: New Jersey's highways have speed limits ranging from 55 mph to 65 mph, and residential streets often have a limit of 25 mph unless otherwise posted. Be mindful of speed limits, as fines for speeding can be high, and law enforcement is generally strict.

Driver Behavior: New Jersey drivers are known for being assertive, but aggressive driving is illegal and can lead to tickets. Always follow traffic rules, signal lane changes, and avoid tailgating.

6. Returning the Car

When returning the rental car, make sure to arrive during the agency's business hours, as most agencies conduct inspections when the car is returned. You'll be charged for any damages, missed fuel, or late returns, so be sure to return the car in the same condition you received it. If you return the car after hours, ensure you follow the return instructions provided by the rental company to avoid additional fees or issues with the return process.

7. Additional Tips for a Smooth Rental Experience

Booking in Advance: For better rates and availability, book your rental car well in advance, especially during peak travel seasons. Prices can increase during holidays or major events in New Jersey, so planning ahead can save you money.

Avoiding Additional Charges: Rental agencies often charge for things like GPS, child seats, and additional drivers. If you don't need them, be sure to decline these extras at the time of booking.

Renting for a Long Stay: If you plan to rent for an extended period, consider asking about weekly or monthly rental rates, as they often offer better value compared to daily rentals.

Ride-Sharing Apps (Uber, Lyft) and Taxis

When you're in New Jersey, getting around is made easier by the availability of ride-sharing apps like Uber and Lyft, as well as traditional taxis. Whether you need a quick ride to the train station, a lift to a restaurant, or a ride back from a night out, these transportation options offer convenience, accessibility, and flexibility. Here's everything you need to know to navigate the ride-sharing and taxi landscape in New Jersey.

Ride-Sharing Apps: Uber and Lyft
Uber and Lyft dominate the ride-sharing scene in New Jersey, with services available in almost every city and many suburban areas. Both apps function similarly, allowing you to book a ride directly from your smartphone. While ride-sharing services are popular in large cities like Jersey City, Hoboken, and Newark, they are also increasingly available in smaller towns and the surrounding areas.

How Ride-Sharing Works
To use Uber or Lyft, you simply download the app, create an account, and enter your destination. Both apps will then show you available vehicles nearby, providing an estimated fare based on the distance, time of day, and demand. You'll be able to track your driver's arrival and view their profile, including ratings and car details. Payment is handled through the app, so you don't have to worry about carrying cash.

Both apps offer various ride options to suit different needs and budgets:

UberX / Lyft Standard: The most affordable ride, typically a 4-door car that can accommodate 3-4 passengers.

UberXL / Lyft XL: Ideal for larger groups or families, these vehicles accommodate up to 6 passengers.

Uber Comfort / Lyft Comfort: These rides offer more spacious and newer cars for a slightly higher price.

Uber Black / Lyft Lux: These are premium options with high-end vehicles and professional drivers for those looking for a more luxurious experience.

Pricing and Surge Charges
The cost of your ride depends on factors such as the type of ride, the distance, and any surge pricing that may be in effect. During peak hours, holidays, or bad weather, you might see surge pricing, which increases the fare due to high demand. The app will notify you if surge pricing is active, allowing you to decide whether to wait or proceed with the ride.

Tips to Save Money:

Ride during off-peak hours: If possible, try to avoid busy times like rush hour, when surge pricing is more common.

Pool Options: Both Uber and Lyft offer "pool" or shared ride options, where you share the car with others going in the same direction. This can lower the price, but it might take longer to get to your destination.

Promo Codes: Both companies frequently offer promotional codes or discounts, which you can apply during checkout.

Availability Across New Jersey
Uber and Lyft are widely available in New Jersey's urban areas like Newark, Jersey City, and Hoboken. In fact, these services often provide a more convenient and economical option than taking a traditional taxi, especially in places where taxis might be less readily available. However, in more rural or less populated areas, you may find that ride-sharing options are less frequent or have longer wait times.

In New Jersey's more suburban regions, including areas along the Jersey Shore and places like Princeton and Cherry Hill, both Uber and Lyft services are widely accessible, especially during the summer months when tourism is at its peak. During this period, demand can be high, but it's typically easy to get a ride during the day or evening.

Taxis in New Jersey: Traditional and Reliable
While ride-sharing apps are incredibly popular, traditional taxis are still a viable and reliable option for getting around New Jersey. You can easily hail a taxi from the curb or book one through an app or by calling a local taxi service. Many taxis can be found at major transit hubs, hotels, and in cities with high foot traffic.

How Taxi Services Work
Taxi fares in New Jersey are regulated by the New Jersey Taxi and Limousine Commission. The fare typically consists of a base rate plus a charge for each mile traveled. Metered taxis are common, and they'll automatically calculate the fare based on the distance and time.

Taxis in New Jersey are often a great option when:

Ride-sharing is unavailable: In more rural areas or during off-peak hours when ride-sharing services may have longer wait times.

You're looking for immediate service: Taxis can be found more readily on the street or at designated taxi stands, especially in cities like Newark or Atlantic City.

Taxi Tips and Pricing
Gratuity: Tipping is customary in taxis, with 10%-15% being the standard. Some taxis also have a tip option on the meter, so you can easily add a tip before paying.

Airport and Hotel Rides: Taxis from airports like Newark Liberty International Airport (EWR) and hotels typically have set rates or can charge by the meter. Check with your driver about the fare before you depart, especially for long-distance trips.

Ride-Sharing vs. Taxis: Which Is Better?
Both ride-sharing apps and traditional taxis have their pros and cons, and the choice largely depends on your preferences, timing, and location.

Convenience: Ride-sharing apps like Uber and Lyft are more convenient in terms of hailing a ride from your phone and tracking your driver in real-time. You can also see the price upfront before confirming the ride. Taxis, on the other hand, may involve waiting on the street or at a designated stand.

Pricing: Ride-sharing services tend to be cheaper than taxis, particularly for short rides or during off-peak hours. However, during surge pricing, Uber or Lyft can be more expensive than traditional taxis. Taxis have a fixed metered fare, so they may be more predictable.

Availability: While taxis are widely available in busy areas like airports or city centers, ride-sharing services can be found in nearly every corner of New Jersey, including smaller suburban towns. If you're in a less densely populated area, ride-sharing apps may be your best option.

Comfort and Cleanliness: Both taxis and ride-sharing services offer clean vehicles, but ride-sharing services like Uber Comfort and Lyft Lux give you the option of choosing newer, more spacious vehicles for a higher price.

WHERE TO STAY

Best Areas to Stay in New Jersey

When planning a trip to New Jersey, choosing the right area to stay can make a significant difference in your experience. The Garden State offers a range of diverse neighborhoods and regions, each with its own character, attractions, and amenities. Whether you're visiting for the beaches, history, or proximity to New York City, here's a guide to some of the best areas to stay in New Jersey, based on different types of travel experiences.

1. Jersey City: Urban and Convenient

If you're looking for easy access to Manhattan without the high cost of staying in New York City, Jersey City is an excellent choice. Located just across the Hudson River from Lower Manhattan, Jersey City offers a range of accommodations, from luxury hotels to budget-friendly options, with spectacular views of the Manhattan skyline.

Why Stay Here:
Proximity to NYC: You can take a quick PATH train or ferry into New York, making it a perfect base for tourists wanting to explore both New Jersey and the city.

Downtown and Waterfront: The waterfront area, particularly Exchange Place, is bustling with restaurants, bars, and cultural attractions. The Liberty Landing Marina offers beautiful views of the Statue of Liberty and access to outdoor parks.

Local Attractions: Visit the Liberty Science Center, Liberty Walk, and Jersey City's historic districts, like Journal Square, which offers a mix of shopping and cultural experiences.

2. Hoboken: Charming and Accessible

For a more relaxed vibe but still with easy access to New York City, Hoboken is a popular choice. Known for its charming streets, waterfront views, and proximity to Manhattan, Hoboken offers a quieter, more residential feel compared to other parts of Jersey City, yet it's only a short train or ferry ride away from the city.

Why Stay Here:
Walkable and Scenic: Hoboken is known for its walkability, featuring tree-lined streets, cafes, and boutiques. The Hoboken Waterfront Walkway offers stunning views of the Manhattan skyline, making it perfect for leisurely strolls.

Nightlife and Dining: Hoboken has a thriving dining scene, offering everything from casual eats to upscale dining, along with plenty of bars and cafes perfect for an evening out.

Proximity to NYC: A 10-minute train ride on the PATH or a short ferry ride connects you to Manhattan, so you can easily spend a day in the city before retreating to the quieter streets of Hoboken in the evening.

3. Princeton: Historic and Academic

For those interested in history, culture, and a more tranquil experience, Princeton is an excellent choice. Home to the prestigious Princeton University, this charming town offers a blend of academic culture, historic architecture, and beautiful green spaces.

Why Stay Here:

Charming Downtown: Princeton's historic downtown area is full of quaint shops, cafes, and art galleries. Nassau Street is lined with boutiques and bookstores, making it a pleasant place for shopping and strolling.

Cultural Attractions: Visit the Princeton University Art Museum, Morven Museum & Garden, and take a walk through the Princeton University campus, known for its beautiful, historic architecture.

Scenic Outdoors: If you're a nature lover, the Marquand Park and Palmer Square provide plenty of green spaces for relaxation, and the nearby Delaware and Raritan Canal State Park offers hiking and biking paths.

4. Atlantic City: Entertainment and Beaches

If you're seeking a more lively atmosphere with access to both entertainment and beach resorts, Atlantic City is the go-to destination. Known for its iconic boardwalk, casinos, and nightlife, Atlantic City offers something for everyone, from gamblers to families and beachgoers.

Why Stay Here:

Casino and Entertainment: Atlantic City is home to world-famous casinos such as Borgata, Caesars, and Hard Rock Hotel & Casino. The city also hosts top-notch concerts, comedy shows, and other live performances.

Beach and Boardwalk: Spend your days relaxing on the beach or strolling along the Atlantic City Boardwalk, where you'll find shops, arcades, and amusement rides.

Affordable Options: Despite its reputation as a luxury resort destination, Atlantic City offers a range of accommodation options, from budget-friendly hotels to upscale resorts.

5. Cape May: Beachfront and Victorian Charm

For a more peaceful, picturesque getaway, Cape May provides a charming mix of beach relaxation and Victorian architecture. Located at the southern tip of New Jersey, Cape May is perfect for couples or families seeking a quiet retreat by the sea.

Why Stay Here:
Historic District: Cape May is known for its well-preserved Victorian homes and historic landmarks. The Cape May Historic District is full of 19th-century buildings and offers tours of grand mansions, like the Emlen Physick Estate.

Beachfront Beauty: Cape May's beaches are some of the most beautiful on the Jersey Shore, offering opportunities for sunbathing, water sports, and scenic walks along the shoreline.

Family-Friendly: The town's quaint, slower pace makes it perfect for families, with attractions like the Cape May County Park & Zoo, as well as boat tours where you can see local wildlife, including dolphins.

6. Long Beach Island: Coastal Retreat
For a more laid-back beach experience, Long Beach Island (LBI) offers miles of pristine coastline, perfect for sunbathing, surfing, and beachcombing. LBI is a popular spot for families, couples, and nature lovers who want a quieter vacation by the sea.

Why Stay Here:
Beautiful Beaches: LBI boasts some of New Jersey's best beaches, with wide sandy stretches ideal for relaxing or water activities like kayaking and paddleboarding.

Small-Town Charm: The island is home to charming seaside towns such as Beach Haven, where you'll find boutique shops, local seafood restaurants, and family-friendly activities.

Nature and Wildlife: If you enjoy nature, LBI offers excellent birdwatching opportunities at places like the Edwin B. Forsythe National Wildlife Refuge, which is perfect for outdoor enthusiasts.

7. Newark: Urban and Affordable
For visitors who want to be close to major metropolitan areas but at a more affordable price point, Newark offers plenty of options. Located just a short train ride away from New York City, Newark is a bustling urban center with a rich history and a growing arts scene.

Why Stay Here:
Proximity to NYC: Newark is ideal for those looking to explore Manhattan but prefer to stay in a more affordable area. The PATH train connects Newark to New York City in just 20 minutes.

Cultural Attractions: Newark is home to the Newark Museum of Art, the Prudential Center, and Branch Brook Park, which features the largest collection of cherry blossoms in the U.S.

Budget-Friendly: Accommodation options in Newark tend to be more affordable compared to New York City, making it an excellent choice for budget-conscious travelers.

Hotels, Resorts, and Vacation Rentals

New Jersey is home to a wide variety of accommodations, from luxurious resorts to cozy vacation rentals, offering something for every type of traveler. Whether you're seeking a beachfront retreat, a family-friendly resort, or a private home for a more personal experience, New Jersey has numerous options that will make your stay memorable. Here's a closer look at some of the best hotels, resorts, and vacation rentals in the state.

Hotels in New Jersey: Convenient and Comfortable Stays
New Jersey boasts a broad selection of hotels that cater to a range of budgets and preferences. From upscale chains to charming boutique hotels, you'll find plenty of choices, particularly in cities like Newark, Jersey City, and Atlantic City, as well as along the Jersey Shore.

The Borgata Hotel Casino & Spa – Atlantic City
Location: 1 Borgata Way, Atlantic City, NJ 08401

Getting There: The Borgata is a 20-minute drive from Atlantic City International Airport (ACY). Taxis and ride-sharing services like Uber are readily available from the airport. If you're coming from Philadelphia, the drive is around 1 hour and 15 minutes via the Garden State Parkway.

Overview: This upscale resort is one of Atlantic City's premier luxury destinations, featuring a sprawling casino, award-winning dining options, and a luxurious spa. Guests can enjoy entertainment in the form of top-notch performances, music, and events at the hotel's venue.

Things to Do: Try your luck at the casino, dine at celebrity chef restaurants like Michael Symon's B Spot, or indulge in a treatment at the Borgata Spa. Don't miss a show at the Borgata Event Center, which hosts concerts and comedy performances throughout the year.

The Westin Jersey City Newport
Location: 479 Washington Blvd, Jersey City, NJ 07310

Getting There: The hotel is just a 15-minute ride from Newark Liberty International Airport (EWR) via taxi or ride-sharing. Hoboken Terminal is only a short distance away, providing access to NYC via the PATH train.

Overview: Located along the waterfront, The Westin Jersey City Newport offers comfortable rooms with panoramic views of the Manhattan skyline and the Hudson River. It's perfect for those who want a peaceful stay with easy access to New York City.

Things to Do: The hotel features a fitness center, an indoor pool, and a riverside walkway for morning jogs. You can take the PATH train into New York City, where you'll find world-class attractions such as Times Square, Central Park, and the Empire State Building.

Hard Rock Hotel & Casino – Atlantic City
Location: 1000 Boardwalk, Atlantic City, NJ 08401

Getting There: Located along the famous Atlantic City Boardwalk, the Hard Rock is accessible via a 20-minute drive from Atlantic City International Airport or a 1.5-hour drive from Philadelphia.

Overview: This iconic hotel blends luxury accommodations with the thrill of a casino. With its music-themed decor, the Hard Rock is ideal for visitors who want to be at the heart of Atlantic City's nightlife and entertainment scene.

Things to Do: Beyond the casino, guests can enjoy live music performances, a wide range of dining options, and the Hard Rock Café. Take a walk along the Boardwalk, or head to the nearby beaches for a day by the ocean.

Resorts in New Jersey: Relax and Recharge
If you're looking for a full-service resort with all the amenities, New Jersey has plenty to offer. These resorts provide everything you need for a relaxing getaway, including spas, pools, golf courses, and fine dining.

Crystal Springs Resort – Hamburg
Location: 1 Wild Turkey Way, Hamburg, NJ 07419

Getting There: About a 1.5-hour drive from Newark Liberty International Airport via Route 23.

Overview: This year-round resort in the scenic Sussex County offers a luxurious and peaceful retreat. With a sprawling 4,000-acre property, Crystal Springs is home to several golf courses, a world-class spa, and a variety of dining options.

Things to Do: Play a round of golf on one of the five championship courses, unwind at the Reflections Spa, or take a swim in the resort's indoor or outdoor pool. If you're visiting in the winter, enjoy skiing at the nearby Mountain Creek Resort.

The Water Club – Atlantic City
Location: 1 Renaissance Way, Atlantic City, NJ 08401

Getting There: The Water Club is located next to the Borgata Hotel and is easily accessible from Atlantic City International Airport by taxi or ride-share.

Overview: This luxury boutique resort within the Borgata complex offers a more intimate, upscale experience. It features stylish rooms with beautiful views of the Atlantic City skyline and bay, as well as access to the resort's spa and exclusive lounges.

Things to Do: Spend your day lounging by the pool or at the spa. Guests also have access to the Borgata's casino, dining options, and entertainment venues. Take a short walk to the Boardwalk for shopping and sightseeing.

Vacation Rentals: Home Away From Home
For travelers looking for a more personalized or long-term stay, vacation rentals offer the flexibility and convenience of having your own space. From beach houses to city apartments, vacation rentals are available throughout New Jersey.

Beach Houses in Long Beach Island
Location: Long Beach Island, NJ

Getting There: Long Beach Island is easily reachable by car from Philadelphia (1.5 hours) or New York City (2 hours). Atlantic City International Airport is around a 1-hour drive away.

Overview: Long Beach Island (LBI) is a beloved coastal destination known for its beautiful beaches, quaint towns, and vibrant atmosphere. Renting a beach house here allows you to have a private escape while being close to the ocean. Rentals range from small cottages to large luxury homes with multiple bedrooms.

Things to Do: Spend your days at the beach, go for a bike ride on the LBI bike path, or visit the Barnegat Lighthouse State Park. LBI also offers plenty of shops, restaurants, and fun events, especially during the summer months.

Luxury Vacation Rentals in Hoboken
Location: Hoboken, NJ

Getting There: Just a short ride from Newark Liberty International Airport, and a 10-minute ride to Manhattan via the PATH train.

Overview: If you're visiting for an extended period and want a comfortable, home-like setting, vacation rentals in Hoboken can be the perfect choice. Options range from chic studio apartments to multi-bedroom lofts with panoramic views of the Manhattan skyline.

Things to Do: Stay in Hoboken for easy access to New York City, but enjoy the charming local cafes, restaurants, and parks along the waterfront. Walk along the Hoboken Waterfront Walkway for stunning views of the city, or enjoy the local culture in Hoboken's many art galleries.

Budget Accommodation Options

When visiting New Jersey on a budget, finding affordable accommodation is key to making the most of your trip without breaking the bank. Fortunately, the state offers a variety of budget-friendly options ranging from affordable hotels to hostels, motels, and vacation rentals. Whether you're exploring the beaches, cities, or rural areas, there are plenty of choices that won't cost you an arm and a leg. Here's a guide to some of the best budget accommodation options in New Jersey.

1. Budget Hotels: Affordable Comfort in Convenient Locations
New Jersey is home to many budget hotels that offer basic amenities, comfort, and convenience, often in central locations close to popular attractions. These budget hotels are perfect for travelers who want to spend more on activities and sightseeing and less on their accommodation.

Red Roof Inn – Newark
Location: 1118-1124 Raymond Blvd, Newark, NJ 07102

Getting There: This budget-friendly hotel is located just 10 minutes from Newark Liberty International Airport and a short ride from New York City via the PATH train.

Overview: The Red Roof Inn offers basic, no-frills rooms with free Wi-Fi, flat-screen TVs, and complimentary coffee. The hotel's location makes it ideal for travelers needing easy access to the airport or for those planning to visit Manhattan without the high price tag.

Things to Do: Explore Branch Brook Park, famous for its cherry blossoms in spring, or take the train into New York City for all the famous landmarks and attractions. The hotel is also close to Prudential Center, home to major sports events and concerts.

Motel 6 – Atlantic City
Location: 2408 Pacific Ave, Atlantic City, NJ 08401

Getting There: This affordable option is just a short drive from Atlantic City's beaches and Boardwalk. The Atlantic City International Airport is a 20-minute ride away by taxi or ride-share.

Overview: Motel 6 offers clean, simple accommodations at an excellent price. Rooms come equipped with basic amenities like air conditioning, free Wi-Fi, and cable TV. The hotel is perfect for visitors looking to enjoy the beaches and casinos without spending a fortune on lodging.

Things to Do: Take a stroll down the famous Atlantic City Boardwalk, try your luck at the Casino Pier, or enjoy a day at the beach. The area also offers excellent dining and nightlife options.

2. Hostels: A Social and Budget-Friendly Option

For travelers who don't mind sharing space and want to meet other visitors, hostels are a fantastic choice. New Jersey has several hostels that cater to budget-conscious travelers looking for an affordable place to sleep.

HI New York City Hostel

Location: 891 Amsterdam Ave, New York, NY 10025 (about a 20-minute train ride into New Jersey)

Getting There: The HI New York City Hostel is located just outside of New Jersey, making it an affordable option for those who want easy access to Manhattan. It's about a 10-minute walk to the 1 train at Columbus Circle, which connects to the PATH train for New Jersey.

Overview: While located in New York City, this hostel is an affordable option for travelers visiting New Jersey, especially if you don't mind a short commute. HI New York offers shared dorm rooms, private rooms, and a vibrant community atmosphere. The hostel provides a full kitchen, free Wi-Fi, and various social events for guests.

Things to Do: From this hostel, you can quickly access iconic New York spots such as Central Park, Times Square, and the Empire State Building. A short train ride into New Jersey will also bring you to top destinations like Hoboken or Jersey City.

The Pod Hotel – Jersey City

Location: 159 Morgan St, Jersey City, NJ 07302

Getting There: A 10-minute walk from Exchange Place station on the PATH train, which connects directly to Manhattan.

Overview: The Pod Hotel is a modern, stylish budget hotel offering compact, clean rooms with minimalist decor. The rooms feature smart design to maximize space, including bunk beds and private rooms with modern amenities. It's a great option for travelers who want to stay in Jersey City but have easy access to New York City.

Things to Do: The hotel is a short walk from the waterfront and offers fantastic views of the Manhattan skyline. Explore Jersey City's waterfront parks or take the PATH train into Manhattan to visit museums, restaurants, and shopping districts.

3. Vacation Rentals: Affordable and Flexible Stays

For a more personalized experience, vacation rentals offer flexibility and can be more affordable for those traveling in groups or planning a longer stay. Sites like Airbnb and Vrbo provide a variety of options ranging from private rooms in local homes to entire apartments or houses.

Beachfront Cottage on Long Beach Island
Location: Long Beach Island, NJ

Getting There: Long Beach Island is easily accessible by car from Philadelphia (1.5 hours) or New York City (2 hours). Atlantic City International Airport is about a 1-hour drive away.

Overview: Renting a small beach house or cottage along Long Beach Island allows for a comfortable and affordable beach getaway. Many properties are within walking distance of the beach and offer full kitchen facilities, making them great for families or small groups.

Things to Do: Long Beach Island boasts miles of unspoiled beaches, perfect for swimming, surfing, or simply relaxing by the water. Visitors can also explore nearby Barnegat Lighthouse State Park or rent bikes to explore the area's scenic paths.

Studio Apartment in Hoboken
Location: Hoboken, NJ

Getting There: A quick PATH train ride from Hoboken into Manhattan or Newark.

Overview: Renting a studio apartment or a small one-bedroom unit in Hoboken provides visitors with a home-like atmosphere, along with full amenities like a kitchen, laundry facilities, and comfortable living space. These rentals are perfect for couples or solo travelers who prefer more privacy and flexibility than a hotel.

Things to Do: Take a walk along the Hoboken Waterfront Walkway with stunning views of Manhattan, visit the local parks, or enjoy a meal at one of the many restaurants and cafes in Hoboken. The PATH train makes it easy to visit New York City for sightseeing, shopping, and dining.

4. Motels: Classic Budget Stays
Motels can be a great budget accommodation option, especially for travelers passing through or those who prefer a simple, no-frills place to stay.

Econo Lodge – North Bergen
Location: 2800 Columbia Ave, North Bergen, NJ 07047

Getting There: Located just a 15-minute drive from Midtown Manhattan and JFK International Airport. You can also take a bus or taxi from Hoboken or Jersey City.

Overview: This budget motel offers basic rooms with convenient amenities, including free parking, Wi-Fi, and breakfast. It's ideal for travelers who want to be close to New York City but at a more affordable price point.

Things to Do: Take advantage of the proximity to New York City, visiting popular landmarks like Times Square, Central Park, and the Statue of Liberty. You're also near Liberty State Park in Jersey City, which offers great views of the Manhattan skyline and the Statue of Liberty.

Unique Stays: Bed & Breakfasts and Historical Inns

When looking for a unique and charming stay in New Jersey, a Bed & Breakfast (B&B) or historical inn offers a warm, personalized experience that larger hotels simply can't match. These accommodations often provide a glimpse into the local culture and history, with cozy rooms, home-cooked breakfasts, and attentive hosts eager to share recommendations for the area. Here's a look at some of the best Bed & Breakfasts and historical inns in New Jersey that offer character, comfort, and a touch of history.

1. The Juliet Hotel – Cape May
Location: 23 Ocean Street, Cape May, NJ 08204

Getting There: The Juliet Hotel is about 1.5 hours south of Atlantic City and a 2-hour drive from Philadelphia. The hotel is also within walking distance from Cape May's beach and shops.

Overview: The Juliet Hotel is a boutique hotel located in the historic district of Cape May, New Jersey's most famous Victorian town. Though it combines the charm of a historical inn with modern amenities, it maintains a distinctive bed-and-breakfast feel. Each room is unique, offering a blend of classic Victorian decor with modern touches.

Things to Do: Cape May is known for its beautiful Victorian architecture, beaches, and birdwatching. Guests can walk to Washington Street Mall for shopping, visit Cape May Lighthouse, or enjoy a romantic evening at Congress Hall, one of the oldest beach resorts in the U.S.

2. The Olde Victorian Inn – Lambertville
Location: 32 N Union Street, Lambertville, NJ 08530

Getting There: A 1-hour drive from Philadelphia and easily accessible from New York City via NJ Transit or car.

Overview: The Olde Victorian Inn is located in the quaint town of Lambertville, across the Delaware River from New Hope, Pennsylvania. This historical inn is housed in a beautiful 19th-century Victorian home and offers a charming mix of antique furnishings and modern conveniences.

Things to Do: Lambertville and New Hope are known for their artsy vibe, antique shops, and fine dining. Stroll through the Delaware Canal State Park, enjoy a river cruise, or visit local art galleries. The inn is also a great spot for exploring the nearby Bowman's Hill Wildflower Preserve or hiking along the Delaware River.

3. The Smithville Inn – Galloway Township
Location: 1 N New York Rd, Galloway Township, NJ 08205

Getting There: A 20-minute drive from Atlantic City, and around 1.5 hours from Philadelphia.

Overview: Located within the Historic Smithville Village, the Smithville Inn is housed in a building that dates back to the 18th century. The inn offers a mix of rustic charm and elegance, with rooms that are full of character and warmth. It's an ideal spot for a relaxing getaway, with beautiful views of the surrounding grounds and a lovely tavern offering hearty meals.

Things to Do: Historic Smithville Village features quaint shops, lakes, and walking trails. Guests can take a stroll through the village or enjoy the Smithville Inn's serene location with picturesque views. The nearby Wharton State Forest offers excellent hiking and kayaking opportunities. The inn is also close to Atlantic City, providing easy access to its famous casinos and beaches.

4. The Inn at the Shore – Belmar
Location: 215 10th Avenue, Belmar, NJ 07719

Getting There: Located just an hour's drive from Newark Liberty International Airport, and 1.5 hours from Philadelphia.

Overview: The Inn at the Shore is a beachside B&B offering modern, comfortable rooms just a few steps from Belmar Beach. Known for its welcoming atmosphere, the inn offers guests a delicious breakfast every morning, and the rooms are beautifully decorated in a laid-back, coastal style. The location is ideal for beachgoers who also want to enjoy local dining and nightlife.

Things to Do: Guests can enjoy Belmar Beach for a day of sunbathing, swimming, and surfing. The inn is also near Spring Lake and Point Pleasant Beach, which are perfect for exploring coastal New Jersey. Belmar is a popular spot for local seafood, so be sure to check out nearby fishing docks for fresh catches of the day.

5. The Inn at MillRace Pond – Hope
Location: 138 E. Mill Road, Hope, NJ 07844

Getting There: About a 1.5-hour drive from New York City and Philadelphia, located in Warren County.

Overview: Set in the Delaware Water Gap National Recreation Area, The Inn at Mill Race Pond is a historic inn offering cozy rooms with rustic charm and scenic views of the surrounding countryside. Built in the 19th century, the inn features a stunning watermill and a pond that adds to its idyllic, peaceful atmosphere.

Things to Do: Enjoy the outdoors by exploring Delaware Water Gap with hiking, fishing, or canoeing along the Delaware River. The area is a haven for nature lovers, with local attractions like The Hope Historical Museum and Jenny Jump State Forest. The inn is also close to The Lakota Wolf Preserve, where visitors can learn about wildlife conservation and interact with wolves.

6. The Carriage House Bed & Breakfast – Cape May

Location: 609 Lafayette St, Cape May, NJ 08204

Getting There: Located 2 miles from Cape May's beach and just over an hour's drive from Atlantic City.

Overview: This charming B&B is housed in a 19th-century Victorian building with original woodwork, offering a cozy and intimate atmosphere. The Carriage House Bed & Breakfast is a perfect place for couples looking for a quiet, romantic getaway in Cape May. With only five rooms, it offers a personal experience with gourmet breakfasts served daily.

Things to Do: Cape May is a delightful destination with its sandy beaches, historic homes, and coastal attractions. Guests can enjoy walking tours of the town, visit Cape May's Victorian Historic District, or take a boat tour to see dolphins and other local wildlife. Don't forget to visit Cape May Point State Park, where you can walk along scenic trails and view the lighthouse.

7. The Rittenhouse Inn – Lambertville

Location: 224 N Union St, Lambertville, NJ 08530

Getting There: A 1.5-hour drive from Philadelphia and a 1-hour drive from New York City.

Overview: The Rittenhouse Inn is a historic and elegant B&B located in the heart of Lambertville. This beautifully restored Victorian house features cozy rooms with antique furnishings and modern amenities. It's ideal for couples or solo travelers looking to relax in a quiet and charming atmosphere.

Things to Do: Lambertville is an artsy, picturesque town full of galleries, antique shops, and cozy cafes. Visit the nearby New Hope, a charming town known for its history and art scene, or take a leisurely walk along the Delaware Canal Towpath. The area is also popular for cycling, hiking, and river activities.

TOP TOURIST ATTRACTIONS

The Jersey Shore: Beaches and Boardwalks

Location: The Jersey Shore stretches along the coastline from Sandy Hook in the north to Cape May in the south.

Getting There: From New York City, you can take a bus or train to Long Branch (1.5 hours), or rent a car and head south on the Garden State Parkway. Atlantic City can be reached in just over an hour from Philadelphia.

Overview: The Jersey Shore is renowned for its wide array of beaches and lively boardwalks. With 130 miles of coastline, the shore features both bustling beach towns like Asbury Park and more relaxed spots like Long Beach Island. Wildwood and Ocean City are two of the most iconic, offering expansive beaches, amusements, and a nostalgic atmosphere.

Things to Do:

Asbury Park: Known for its arts scene, you can visit The Stone Pony, a legendary music venue. The boardwalk offers shops, restaurants, and arcades, as well as the Silverball Museum for vintage pinball enthusiasts.

Wildwood: Famous for its retro vibe, the boardwalk features classic amusement rides like the Ferris Wheel and the Wildebeest Water Park.

Long Beach Island: Ideal for a quieter beach experience, with opportunities for water sports, kayaking, and biking along the coastline.

Liberty State Park: Views of the Statue of Liberty

Location: Liberty State Park, Jersey City, NJ 07305

Getting There: The park is located just a few minutes from Newark Liberty International Airport (EWR) and is easily accessible from Jersey City by car or PATH train. From Manhattan, take the Liberty Landing Ferry.

Overview: Liberty State Park offers stunning views of the Statue of Liberty and the New York Harbor. It is the perfect spot to relax while enjoying a breathtaking view of Manhattan's skyline and Ellis Island. The park is home to several memorials, including the Liberty Walk and Central Railroad of New Jersey Terminal, also known as the Liberty Landing Ferry Terminal.

Things to Do:

Liberty Walk: A scenic path along the waterfront with amazing views of the Statue of Liberty and the Manhattan skyline.

Liberty Landing Marina: Perfect for a leisurely stroll or a meal at one of the waterfront restaurants.

Liberty Landing Ferry: Hop on a ferry for a short ride to Ellis Island and the Statue of Liberty for a tour.

Liberty Science Center: Great for families, offering interactive exhibits and a large IMAX theater.

Princeton University & Princeton's Historic District

Location: Princeton, NJ 08540

Getting There: Princeton is accessible by car from Philadelphia (about 1 hour) or New York City (about 1.5 hours). Princeton Junction Station is served by NJ Transit and offers a quick ride into Manhattan.

Overview: Princeton University is one of the most prestigious universities in the U.S., located in a charming town full of history. The Princeton University campus itself is an architectural masterpiece, with iconic buildings like Nassau Hall and University Chapel. The historic district surrounding the campus offers an inviting atmosphere, with boutique shops, cafes, and art galleries.

Things to Do:

Princeton University Art Museum: A small but excellent museum that houses European, Asian, and American art.

Nassau Hall: Take a tour of the oldest building on campus, which served as the U.S. capital during the Revolutionary War.

Princeton Battlefield State Park: A historical site that commemorates the Battle of Princeton in 1777.

Morven Museum & Garden: A former governor's mansion, now a museum offering insights into New Jersey's colonial and Revolutionary War history.

Atlantic City: Casinos, Boardwalk, and Nightlife

Location: Atlantic City, NJ 08401

Getting There: Located on the Jersey Shore, Atlantic City is 1.5 hours by car from Philadelphia or 2.5 hours from New York City. Atlantic City International Airport (ACY) serves both domestic and international flights.

Overview: Atlantic City is best known for its historic Boardwalk, casinos, and vibrant nightlife. This seaside city has long been a popular destination for those looking for entertainment, whether it's gambling, live shows, or simply relaxing on the beach.

Things to Do:

The Boardwalk: Take a stroll along the historic Atlantic City Boardwalk, which features iconic landmarks like the Steel Pier and a variety of shops, restaurants, and arcades.

Casinos: Atlantic City is home to famous casinos such as Caesars Atlantic City, Borgata, and Tropicana, which offer a wide range of gaming options and entertainment.

Nightlife: Atlantic City is a hotspot for nightlife, with numerous bars, clubs, and music venues. Try your luck at The Pool After Dark at Harrah's Resort, or check out live performances at The Borgata Event Center.

Beaches: Relax on the wide, sandy beaches or take a swim in the ocean. Some casinos offer exclusive beach access for their guests.

The Delaware Water Gap National Recreation Area

Location: Between New Jersey and Pennsylvania along the Delaware River

Getting There: The park is about a 1.5-hour drive from New York City via Interstate 80 and Route 46. From Philadelphia, it's about a 2-hour drive. There are also buses and trains to nearby towns like Stroudsburg.

Overview: This 70,000-acre national recreation area offers a stunning mix of forested mountains, river views, and cascading waterfalls. A haven for outdoor enthusiasts, the Delaware Water Gap National Recreation Area is a great place to hike, camp, kayak, and more.

Things to Do:

Hiking: The park has over 100 miles of trails, including the Appalachian Trail and the popular Dunnfield Creek Trail, which leads to the scenic Buttermilk Falls.

Kayaking and Canoeing: The Delaware River is perfect for kayaking, canoeing, or tubing. Rentals are available at various points along the river.

Camping: There are numerous campgrounds in the area, including Worthington State Forest and Millbrook Village for an authentic wilderness experience.

Wildlife Viewing: The area is home to diverse wildlife, including deer, wild turkeys, and various bird species.

The Thomas Edison National Historical Park

Location: 211 Main St, West Orange, NJ 07052

Getting There: The park is about a 30-minute drive from Newark Liberty International Airport and 1 hour from New York City by car or train.

Overview: This historic site preserves the home and laboratory of Thomas Edison, one of America's most famous inventors. The Thomas Edison National Historical Park includes Edison's Glenmont Estate and his laboratory, where he created groundbreaking inventions such as the phonograph and the light bulb.

Things to Do:

Visit Edison's Laboratory: Take a guided tour of the laboratory complex to see where Edison worked on his famous inventions. Exhibits showcase his experiments, equipment, and prototypes.

Explore Glenmont Estate: Explore Glenmont, Edison's home, which retains much of its original furnishings. The estate is set in beautiful gardens, perfect for a stroll.

Educational Programs: Participate in interactive exhibits and educational programs designed to showcase Edison's genius and impact on modern technology.

Adventure Aquarium in Camden

Location: 1 Riverside Drive, Camden, NJ 08103

Getting There: Adventure Aquarium is just a 5-minute drive from Philadelphia across the Benjamin Franklin Bridge. It is easily accessible by car, public transit, or water taxi.

Overview: The Adventure Aquarium is one of the largest and most interactive aquariums in the U.S. It features exhibits on marine life from around the world, including sharks, stingrays, and sea turtles, as well as a variety of educational programs for visitors of all ages.

Things to Do:

Shark Bridge: Walk across the Shark Bridge, which allows visitors to walk over the shark tank and get a close-up view of these majestic creatures.

African Penguins: Visit the Penguin Island and watch over 80 African penguins play in their habitat.

Touch Tanks: Engage with marine life in the touch tanks, where visitors can touch stingrays, starfish, and other sea creatures.

4D Theater: Enjoy a thrilling 4D movie experience featuring underwater adventures and wildlife.

DINING IN NEW JERSEY

Must-Try New Jersey Foods: Pork Roll, Salt Water Taffy, and More

New Jersey is known for its diverse food culture, blending influences from the shore, the cities, and the rich farming areas. If you're visiting the state, there are some iconic foods you simply cannot miss. Here's a guide to the must-try foods in New Jersey:

Pork Roll (or Taylor Ham)
What It Is: A beloved breakfast meat, often compared to Canadian bacon, but with a unique flavor. It's usually served on a roll (a sandwich bun) with eggs and cheese.

Where to Try It: Ralph's Italian Ice in Point Pleasant and The Sandwich Shop in Trenton both serve this local favorite.

Getting There: Ralph's is located at 405 Washington Ave, Point Pleasant, NJ, and is a 1.5-hour drive from New York City and 1-hour from Philadelphia.

Things to Do: Point Pleasant is a coastal town with a beautiful beach and boardwalk, perfect for a relaxed day of sightseeing and dining.

Salt Water Taffy
What It Is: A chewy, colorful candy made from sugar, cornstarch, salt, water, butter, and flavoring. It's traditionally associated with Atlantic City.

Where to Try It: Visit Shriver's Salt Water Taffy at 9 Boardwalk, Atlantic City, NJ for an authentic taste.

Getting There: Shriver's is located directly on the Atlantic City Boardwalk, a short drive from Atlantic City International Airport.

Things to Do: After getting your taffy fix, take a stroll down the Atlantic City Boardwalk, explore the casinos, or relax on the beach.

Disco Fries
What It Is: A Jersey take on poutine, consisting of French fries topped with brown gravy and melted mozzarella cheese.

Where to Try It: Try this comfort food at The Red Store in Cape May or White Mana in Jersey City.

Getting There: White Mana is located at 470 Tonnele Ave, Jersey City, NJ, just a 20-minute train ride from New York City.

Things to Do: After indulging in your disco fries, walk along the Jersey City Waterfront for stunning views of Manhattan, or visit Liberty State Park for outdoor activities.

Best Restaurants for Every Budget

Whether you're craving high-end dining, a casual bite, or something in-between, New Jersey has a wide variety of dining options that cater to all budgets. Here are a few top recommendations:

High-End: Blue Morel – Morristown
Location: 2 Whippany Rd, Morristown, NJ 07960

Getting There: A 40-minute drive from Newark Liberty International Airport or a 1-hour train ride from New York City.

Overview: Blue Morel offers a refined dining experience, known for its seasonally inspired dishes and exquisite wine list. The restaurant is located inside the Westin Governor Morris Hotel and is perfect for those seeking a special evening.

Things to Do: After your meal, take a stroll around Morristown Green or visit the Morristown National Historical Park for a glimpse into New Jersey's Revolutionary War history.

Mid-Range: The Farm and Fisherman Tavern – Cherry Hill
Location: 1442 Marlton Pike E, Cherry Hill, NJ 08034

Getting There: About 20 minutes from Philadelphia by car.

Overview: This farm-to-table restaurant offers fresh, locally sourced dishes with creative twists. From seasonal vegetables to locally raised meats, it's a great spot for those who enjoy quality food in a relaxed atmosphere.

Things to Do: Cherry Hill is home to several shopping malls, including Cherry Hill Mall, one of the largest in the state. You can also explore nearby Clementon Park & Splash World for family-friendly fun.

Budget-Friendly: Di Lorenzo's – Trenton
Location: 1503 Parkway Ave, Trenton, NJ 08628

Getting There: 1-hour drive from Philadelphia and just over 1.5 hours from New York City.

Overview: Di Lorenzo's is known for serving some of the best pizza in New Jersey, particularly their Trenton tomato pie—a thin crust pizza topped with fresh tomato sauce, cheese, and basil. It's a local favorite and a must-try for pizza lovers.

Things to Do: Trenton is known for its rich history. After grabbing a slice, visit the New Jersey State Museum, State House, or stroll along the Delaware River.

Food Festivals & Events

New Jersey is home to a variety of food festivals throughout the year, where you can sample the best the state has to offer. Here are a few festivals that any food lover should attend:

The Atlantic City Food & Wine Festival
Location: Atlantic City, NJ

When: Usually held in July each year.

Overview: The Atlantic City Food & Wine Festival draws top chefs, sommeliers, and food lovers from around the country for a weekend of gourmet food and drink. Events include tasting sessions, celebrity chef dinners, and cooking classes.

Things to Do: When you're not attending the festival, explore Atlantic City's casinos, walk along the Boardwalk, or take a day trip to the Cape May Lighthouse.

The New Jersey VegFest – Edison
Location: 97 Sunfield Ave, Edison, NJ 08837

When: Annually in April.

Overview: This plant-based festival is the largest of its kind in New Jersey. It celebrates vegan food, wellness, and sustainability. You'll find food vendors offering everything from vegan tacos to plant-based ice cream, along with cooking demos and health talks.

Things to Do: Edison is also home to the Thomas Edison National Historical Park, where you can learn about the famous inventor's contributions to modern technology.

The New Jersey Seafood Festival – Belmar
Location: Belmar, NJ 07719

When: Usually held in June.

Overview: This festival is a seafood lover's dream, showcasing New Jersey's rich maritime heritage with freshly caught seafood and local delicacies. You can sample clam chowder, lobster rolls, and fried fish while enjoying live music and waterfront views.

Things to Do: After the festival, enjoy the sunny Belmar Beach or walk along the Belmar Boardwalk.

Vegan and Vegetarian-Friendly Options

New Jersey's culinary scene has evolved to include a wide variety of plant-based dining options, from upscale vegan restaurants to casual eateries. Here are a few spots to check out:

Planted Plate – Montclair

Location: 159 Valley Rd, Montclair, NJ 07042

Getting There: A 1-hour drive from New York City or a 30-minute drive from Newark.

Overview: Planted Plate offers fresh, vegan and gluten-free dishes made from locally sourced ingredients. The menu is a rotating selection of seasonal fare, making it a go-to spot for those seeking healthy and delicious plant-based meals.

Things to Do: Montclair has a rich arts scene, with plenty of galleries, theaters, and public events. Check out the Montclair Art Museum or catch a performance at The Wellmont Theater.

Marty's V Burger – Jersey City

Location: 350 Warren St, Jersey City, NJ 07302

Getting There: A 15-minute ride from Manhattan on the PATH train.

Overview: For an affordable, fast-casual vegan experience, Marty's V Burger in Jersey City serves a variety of plant-based burgers, fries, and shakes. The menu is fully vegan, with everything from avocado and bacon to cheese (all plant-based, of course).

Things to Do: After a satisfying meal, explore Jersey City's waterfront, which offers stunning views of the Statue of Liberty and Manhattan.

SHOPPING IN NEW JERSEY

Top Shopping Malls and Outlets in New Jersey

New Jersey is home to a variety of shopping malls and outlet centers that cater to all tastes, whether you're looking for luxury brands, trendy boutiques, or discounted deals. Here's a guide to some of the top shopping destinations in the state:

1. The Mall at Short Hills
Location: 1200 Morris Turnpike, Short Hills, NJ 07078

Getting There: Located about 20 miles west of New York City, the mall is easily accessible by car via Interstate 78. Short Hills Station is nearby, offering train service to Manhattan.

Overview: The Mall at Short Hills is New Jersey's most luxurious shopping destination, featuring high-end brands like Louis Vuitton, Tiffany & Co., and Gucci. With over 150 stores, this upscale mall also offers an excellent selection of dining options.

Things to Do: After shopping, relax at one of the mall's fine dining restaurants, like The Capital Grille or Nobu, or catch a movie at the AMC Short Hills 12.

2. Westfield Garden State Plaza
Location: 1 Garden State Plaza Blvd, Paramus, NJ 07652

Getting There: Just 12 miles from New York City, Westfield Garden State Plaza is easily accessible via Route 17. The Paramus Park Mall bus stop is nearby, making public transport a convenient option.

Overview: This is one of New Jersey's largest malls, featuring both luxury and affordable retailers, such as Apple, Macy's, H&M, and Nordstrom. It also has a variety of restaurants, a large food court, and a state-of-the-art movie theater.

Things to Do: Enjoy a shopping spree and then head to Riverside Square for more dining and entertainment, or explore nearby attractions like Van Saun County Park.

3. Jersey Gardens Outlet Mall
Location: 651 Kapkowski Rd, Elizabeth, NJ 07201

Getting There: A 25-minute drive from Newark Liberty International Airport or 40 minutes from Manhattan via the New Jersey Turnpike.

Overview: This is New Jersey's largest outlet mall, offering deep discounts on a wide range of brands such as Nike, Coach, Calvin Klein, and Michael Kors. With over 200 stores, you can shop for everything from clothing to home goods.

Things to Do: The mall has plenty of dining options, including food court staples and sit-down restaurants. After shopping, visit nearby Liberty State Park or the Statue of Liberty for some sightseeing.

Antique and Flea Markets in New Jersey

New Jersey is a haven for antique lovers and bargain hunters, offering numerous flea markets and antique shops where you can find unique treasures, vintage items, and collectibles.

1. Brimfield Antiques Market
Location: 2425 W. State Rd, Brimfield, NJ 06234

Getting There: A 2-hour drive from Philadelphia and 2.5 hours from New York City. Located off Route 20.

Overview: The Brimfield Antiques Market is one of New Jersey's largest antique markets, attracting dealers and collectors from around the country. You can find everything from vintage furniture to rare collectibles, jewelry, and art pieces.

Things to Do: Beyond shopping for antiques, visitors can enjoy the Brimfield Antique Show in the spring and fall, and explore nearby historical sites like the Brimfield Historical Society.

2. Englishtown Auction Sales
Location: 90 Wilson Ave, Englishtown, NJ 07726

Getting There: Located about 1 hour from Philadelphia and New York City by car. It's easily accessible via the Garden State Parkway.

Overview: Englishtown Auction Sales is one of the largest indoor and outdoor flea markets in the region, with over 100 vendors selling antiques, vintage goods, and secondhand items. It's perfect for treasure hunters looking for deals.

Things to Do: Shop for antiques, secondhand clothing, and quirky items. The auction is held on Saturdays and Sundays, making it an ideal weekend activity. Six Flags Great Adventure is nearby for family-friendly fun.

3. The Red Bank Farmers & Flea Market
Location: 91 Monmouth St, Red Bank, NJ 07701

Getting There: Located about an hour from New York City by car, and easily accessible via NJ Transit from Manhattan.

Overview: This charming flea market in Red Bank is known for its vintage finds, antiques, and locally made goods. It also features local produce, baked goods, and unique crafts from local artisans.

Things to Do: After shopping, explore the vibrant downtown Red Bank area with its boutique stores, restaurants, and theaters. Count Basie Theater offers live performances, including concerts and shows.

Local Souvenirs and Crafts in New Jersey

Whether you're looking for a one-of-a-kind gift or something to remember your trip by, New Jersey offers a wide variety of local souvenirs and crafts that reflect its diverse culture and history.

1. New Jersey Local Crafts at The Arts and Crafts Festival – Lambertville
Location: Lambertville, NJ 08530

Getting There: A 1-hour drive from Philadelphia and 1.5 hours from New York City.

Overview: The Arts and Crafts Festival in Lambertville is an annual event featuring works by local artisans. You can find handmade jewelry, pottery, textiles, and paintings that reflect the creative spirit of New Jersey.

Things to Do: Explore Lambertville's historic town with its charming shops and galleries. Cross the Delaware River to visit New Hope, a picturesque town full of art galleries and antique shops.

2. New Jersey Pottery at Howell Living History Farm
Location: 70 Woodens Ln, Lambertville, NJ 08530

Getting There: 1-hour drive from Philadelphia and 1.5 hours from New York City.

Overview: Howell Living History Farm offers visitors the chance to experience 19th-century farm life, including pottery-making demonstrations. You can purchase locally crafted pottery, wooden goods, and other traditional crafts.

Things to Do: Take a guided tour of the farm, where you'll learn about farming techniques, vintage tools, and sustainable living practices. The farm also hosts special events and educational programs for families.

3. The Jersey Shore's Local Crafts and Souvenirs – Beach Haven
Location: 517 N Bay Ave, Beach Haven, NJ 08008

Getting There: Long Beach Island is about 2 hours from Philadelphia or New York City via Garden State Parkway.

Overview: Beach Haven on Long Beach Island is home to a variety of local shops that sell unique souvenirs like handmade jewelry, beach-themed decor, and local art. The Surflight Theatre also offers locally-inspired arts and crafts.

Things to Do: Enjoy a day at Long Beach Island's beautiful beaches, take a stroll along the LBI Historical Museum, or visit the nearby Barnegat Lighthouse State Park for panoramic views.

New Jersey Travel Guide 2025

OUTDOOR ADVENTURES

Hiking and Nature Trails in New Jersey

New Jersey is a state rich in natural beauty, offering a variety of hiking trails and outdoor activities for all levels of experience. Whether you're seeking serene woodland paths or challenging mountain climbs, New Jersey's parks and nature preserves provide numerous opportunities for exploration.

1. Delaware Water Gap National Recreation Area
Location: Between New Jersey and Pennsylvania along the Delaware River

Getting There: About 1.5 hours from New York City via Interstate 80 and Route 46. From Philadelphia, it's a 2-hour drive.

Overview: This sprawling park offers over 100 miles of hiking trails, ranging from easy walks to challenging hikes. Dunnfield Creek Trail leads to Buttermilk Falls, while the Appalachian Trail runs through the area, offering stunning views of the Delaware River.

Things to Do: Explore the natural beauty of the park with hiking, fishing, or canoeing along the river. In addition to the trails, Millbrook Village is a restored historic village, perfect for history buffs.

2. High Point State Park
Location: 1480 State Rt. 23, Sussex, NJ 07461

Getting There: About 1.5 hours from New York City via Interstate 80.

Overview: Known for its panoramic views, High Point State Park is home to the highest point in New Jersey. The Monument Trail leads to the High Point Monument, where you can see three states—New Jersey, Pennsylvania, and New York.

Things to Do: Hike to the monument, swim in the park's lake, or picnic in the lush wooded areas. Winter brings opportunities for snowshoeing and cross-country skiing.

3. Watchung Reservation
Location: 452 New Providence Rd, Mountainside, NJ 07092

Getting There: 45-minute drive from New York City and Newark Liberty International Airport.

Overview: Watchung Reservation offers over 13 miles of trails through forested areas, lakes, and open fields. It's great for beginners and families, with easy loops and well-marked paths.

Things to Do: Take a walk around Lake Surprise, hike along the Red Trail, and visit the Trailside Nature & Science Center to learn about the local wildlife and history of the area.

Beaches and Water Sports in New Jersey

New Jersey is famous for its extensive coastline, with a range of beaches offering everything from water sports to quiet relaxation. If you're a fan of the ocean, you won't be disappointed by the variety of beach activities available.

1. Wildwood Beach
Location: Wildwood, NJ 08260

Getting There: 2-hour drive from Philadelphia and about 2.5 hours from New York City via Garden State Parkway.

Overview: Wildwood is home to wide, sandy beaches, perfect for swimming, surfing, or just soaking up the sun. The area is famous for its boardwalk, packed with rides, arcades, and fun attractions.

Things to Do: Rent a surfboard, try parasailing, or simply relax on the beach. Afterward, visit the Wildwood Boardwalk for amusement rides or Morey's Piers for an afternoon of thrills.

2. Point Pleasant Beach
Location: 300 Ocean Ave, Point Pleasant Beach, NJ 08742

Getting There: 1.5-hour drive from New York City and Philadelphia.

Overview: Point Pleasant Beach is a family-friendly destination with calm waters perfect for swimming and a classic boardwalk for arcade games, restaurants, and shopping.

Things to Do: Rent jet skis, take a boat ride, or enjoy the Point Pleasant Beach Jenkinson's Boardwalk. Visit the Jenkinson's Aquarium or explore Bay Head Beach for a quieter escape.

3. Long Beach Island
Location: Long Beach Island, NJ

Getting There: 1.5-hour drive from Philadelphia or New York City via Garden State Parkway.

Overview: Long Beach Island (LBI) is known for its pristine beaches and water sports. Whether you're into kayaking, paddleboarding, or kite surfing, LBI has something for every water enthusiast.

Things to Do: Take surfing lessons at Surf City, go kayaking or paddleboarding, or just enjoy the unspoiled beach at Holgate. Afterward, head to the Barnegat Lighthouse State Park for panoramic views of the coastline.

Amusement Parks: Six Flags Great Adventure

Location: 1 Six Flags Blvd, Jackson, NJ 08527

Getting There: Located 1 hour from Philadelphia and about 1.5 hours from New York City by car via the Garden State Parkway.

Overview: Six Flags Great Adventure is one of the largest and most popular amusement parks in New Jersey, known for its thrilling rides, including the Kingda Ka, the world's tallest roller coaster. The park also features a water park, animal safari, and family-friendly attractions.

Things to Do:

Rides: From high-speed roller coasters like El Toro to the Superman Ultimate Flight, thrill-seekers will find plenty of excitement.

Safari: The Wild Safari Animal Park allows guests to get up close to animals from around the world, including giraffes, lions, and zebras.

Water Park: Cool off in the summer at the Hurricane Harbor, which includes wave pools, water slides, and lazy rivers.

Ski Resorts and Winter Sports in New Jersey

Though New Jersey may not have the towering mountains of Vermont or Colorado, it still offers great opportunities for winter sports, including skiing, snowboarding, and snowshoeing.

1. Mountain Creek Resort
Location: 200 Route 94, Vernon Township, NJ 07462

Getting There: About a 1.5-hour drive from New York City.

Overview: Mountain Creek Resort is New Jersey's premier ski destination, featuring slopes for all skill levels. With snowboarding, skiing, and tubing, it's a great place to enjoy winter sports close to the city.

Things to Do: Ski and snowboard on the resort's 9 slopes and 8 lifts. Snow tubing is also a popular option. The resort has plenty of dining options and cozy lodges to relax after a day on the slopes.

2. Campgaw Mountain Reservation
Location: 200 Campgaw Rd, Mahwah, NJ 07430

Getting There: Located about 1 hour from New York City via Route 17.

Overview: Campgaw Mountain is a smaller resort, perfect for beginners or those looking for a more relaxed experience. It offers skiing, snowboarding, and tubing.

Things to Do: If you're new to winter sports, this is a great place to learn how to ski or snowboard. The resort also offers a snow tubing hill, which is fun for all ages.

3. Blue Mountain Ski Area
Location: 1660 Blue Mountain Dr, Palmerton, PA 18071

Getting There: About 1.5 hours from New Jersey.

Overview: Located just across the state line in Pennsylvania, Blue Mountain is the closest large resort for New Jersey residents. It's known for having some of the most challenging runs in the region, with terrain for experienced skiers and snowboarders.

Things to Do: Explore Blue Mountains 39 slopes and enjoy night skiing, which is perfect for those looking to extend their day on the mountain. The resort also offers snowshoeing, tubing, and a cozy lodge with great dining options.

NIGHTLIFE AND ENTERTAINMENT

Best Bars and Pubs in New Jersey

New Jersey offers an exciting nightlife scene, with a wide variety of bars, pubs, and taverns ranging from cozy spots perfect for a quiet drink to lively venues with games, dancing, and entertainment. Whether you're looking for craft beer, signature cocktails, or a classic pub experience, New Jersey has something for everyone.

1. The Asbury Park Brewery – Asbury Park
Location: 810 3rd Ave, Asbury Park, NJ 07712

Getting There: A 1.5-hour drive from New York City or Philadelphia via Garden State Parkway.

Overview: The Asbury Park Brewery is one of the most popular craft breweries in the state, known for its innovative beers and vibrant atmosphere. The brewery offers a wide variety of craft brews, from IPAs to stouts, and often hosts food trucks and live music.

Things to Do: Enjoy a cold brew while exploring Asbury Park's boardwalk, checking out live performances at The Stone Pony, or exploring the artsy shops and galleries around town.

2. The Shannon – Hoboken
Location: 106 1st St, Hoboken, NJ 07030

Getting There: Just a 10-minute walk from Hoboken Terminal and a short PATH train ride from Manhattan.

Overview: This Irish pub is a local favorite in Hoboken, offering a cozy setting with traditional Irish drinks, including Guinness and whiskey. It's also known for its vibrant atmosphere, friendly service, and excellent pub food.

Things to Do: Visit Hoboken's waterfront for beautiful views of the Manhattan skyline or take a walk through Washington Street, which is lined with great restaurants, shops, and cafes.

3. The Beer Garden – Jersey City
Location: 1 Distillery Dr, Jersey City, NJ 07302

Getting There: 10-minute walk from Exchange Place Station, accessible by PATH train.

Overview: Located right on the Jersey City Waterfront, The Beer Garden is a relaxed spot with a large outdoor patio, perfect for enjoying a drink while taking in the view of the Statue of Liberty. The bar offers an impressive selection of craft beers and cocktails.

Things to Do: After a drink, take a stroll along the waterfront or visit the nearby Liberty Landing Marina for shopping and dining options.

Live Music Venues and Clubs

New Jersey has a thriving live music scene with venues ranging from intimate spots hosting local talent to large arenas bringing in international acts. Whether you're into rock, jazz, hip-hop, or country, you'll find a place to enjoy live performances.

1. The Stone Pony – Asbury Park
Location: 913 Ocean Ave, Asbury Park, NJ 07712

Getting There: 1.5-hour drive from New York City via Garden State Parkway.

Overview: Known for its iconic reputation in the music world, The Stone Pony is a legendary venue that has hosted artists like Bruce Springsteen and Bon Jovi. It's a must-visit for any music lover, offering live performances in an intimate, casual setting.

Things to Do: After catching a show, explore Asbury Park's boardwalk, where you'll find shops, arcades, and a mix of restaurants and bars with a retro feel.

2. Count Basie Center for the Arts – Red Bank
Location: 99 Monmouth St, Red Bank, NJ 07701

Getting There: A 1-hour drive from New York City and Philadelphia via Garden State Parkway.

Overview: The Count Basie Center for the Arts is an iconic venue that hosts everything from jazz performances to Broadway shows. It's a beautiful historic theater with world-class acoustics, offering a range of events throughout the year.

Things to Do: Explore the downtown area of Red Bank, which offers boutique shopping, galleries, and restaurants. Red Bank RiverCenter offers seasonal events, including outdoor concerts in the summer.

3. The Wellmont Theater – Montclair

Location: 5 Seymour St, Montclair, NJ 07042

Getting There: 1-hour drive from New York City via Interstate 280.

Overview: This historic venue hosts a wide range of live performances, from concerts to comedy shows. The Wellmont Theater has a great atmosphere for enjoying live music, with an intimate setting for fans to get up close to their favorite artists.

Things to Do: After the show, check out the local dining spots in Montclair or visit Montclair Art Museum for a dose of culture.

Atlantic City: Casinos and Shows

Location: Atlantic City, NJ 08401

Getting There: 1.5-hour drive from Philadelphia and 2.5 hours from New York City via Garden State Parkway. Atlantic City International Airport (ACY) serves both domestic and international flights.

Overview: Atlantic City is the go-to destination for gamblers and entertainment lovers in New Jersey. Known for its vibrant casinos, iconic boardwalk, and world-class shows, it's a bustling hub of nightlife and excitement. The city's casinos, including Borgata, Caesars, and Tropicana, feature thousands of slot machines, table games, and poker rooms.

Things to Do:

Casinos: Try your luck at iconic casinos like Borgata, Caesars Atlantic City, or Tropicana. These casinos offer a mix of gaming options, from slots to blackjack and roulette.

Shows: Atlantic City hosts top-tier entertainment at venues like The Music Box and Boardwalk Hall, where you can catch performances by big-name artists, comedians, and Broadway-style shows.

The Boardwalk: Spend time walking the Atlantic City Boardwalk, which is lined with shops, arcades, restaurants, and bars. It's a fun spot for people-watching, dining, and taking in the beach views.

Beaches: Atlantic City is also home to long stretches of sandy beaches, perfect for lounging or taking part in water activities like jet skiing or parasailing.

CULTURAL ATTRACTIONS

Museums to Visit in New Jersey

New Jersey boasts a rich history, diverse culture, and thriving arts scene, which is beautifully reflected in its array of museums. From science and history to art and culture, the museums in New Jersey offer something for everyone.

1. New Jersey State Museum – Trenton
Location: 205 West State Street, Trenton, NJ 08625

Getting There: A 1-hour drive from Philadelphia and just over 1.5 hours from New York City via Interstate 95. It's also accessible via NJ Transit.

Overview: The New Jersey State Museum is a comprehensive museum featuring exhibits on New Jersey's history, culture, and natural science. The museum showcases a vast collection, including prehistoric artifacts, Native American history, and early colonial relics. The Planetarium offers interactive science and astronomy shows.

Things to Do: Explore the New Jersey History Gallery, which covers everything from Native American cultures to the state's industrial development. The art gallery features both contemporary and historical artwork. Don't miss the Planetarium, which offers an immersive experience of the stars and planets.

2. The Morris Museum – Morristown
Location: 6 Normandy Heights Rd, Morristown, NJ 07960

Getting There: Located 45 minutes west of New York City, accessible by NJ Transit or a 1-hour drive from Newark.

Overview: The Morris Museum is a cultural gem that blends art, history, and science. It features diverse exhibits, from dinosaur fossils and local history to contemporary art and cultural artifacts. The museum's collection of mechanical musical instruments is particularly unique and worth exploring.

Things to Do: Visit the F.M. Kirby Gallery for fine art exhibits, or explore the interactive Science Gallery for hands-on learning. The Bickford Theatre within the museum hosts a variety of live performances and events throughout the year.

Performing Arts: Theatres and Music Venues

New Jersey offers an array of theatres and music venues that showcase a wide range of performances, from Broadway shows to local productions and live concerts. Whether you're into theater, comedy, or live music, there's something for everyone.

1. The Paper Mill Playhouse – Millburn
Location: 22 Brookside Dr, Millburn, NJ 07041

Getting There: A 1-hour drive from New York City via Garden State Parkway.

Overview: The Paper Mill Playhouse is one of the state's premier regional theaters. Known for producing high-quality Broadway-caliber shows, it offers a variety of performances, including musicals, plays, and family-friendly shows. The theatre has a rich history and continues to draw big-name talent.

Things to Do: Attend one of the Broadway-style performances, or visit nearby South Mountain Reservation for a scenic hike. After the show, enjoy a meal at one of the many fine dining options in Millburn.

2. Count Basie Center for the Arts – Red Bank
Location: 99 Monmouth St, Red Bank, NJ 07701

Getting There: About 1-hour drive from New York City and Philadelphia.

Overview: The Count Basie Center for the Arts is a historic venue that hosts a variety of performances, from jazz concerts and Broadway shows to classical music and comedy. Named after the legendary jazz musician Count Basie, the theater has maintained its status as a hub for live music and performing arts.

Things to Do: Attend one of the live shows or concerts at the Count Basie Center, then head out for a stroll around Red Bank's downtown, known for its boutique shops, cafes, and art galleries. Red Bank RiverCenter offers additional entertainment options, including outdoor concerts and events.

3. The Wellmont Theater – Montclair
Location: 5 Seymour St, Montclair, NJ 07042

Getting There: 1-hour drive from New York City via Interstate 280.

Overview: The Wellmont Theater is a historic venue known for hosting live concerts, Broadway performances, and comedy shows. With a rich history dating back to 1922, the theater has been renovated to offer modern amenities while preserving its charming, vintage atmosphere.

Things to Do: Attend a concert or Broadway-style show, then explore Montclair, known for its lively arts scene. Check out the Montclair Art Museum or visit one of the many local cafes and restaurants.

Historic Landmarks and Districts in New Jersey

New Jersey is rich in history, and its historic landmarks and districts offer a glimpse into the past. From colonial-era buildings to sites commemorating pivotal moments in American history, New Jersey's landmarks are fascinating to explore.

1. Liberty State Park – Jersey City
Location: Liberty Landing Marina, Jersey City, NJ 07305

Getting There: 15-minute drive from Newark Liberty International Airport and Manhattan. Accessible by PATH train from Jersey City.

Overview: Liberty State Park is one of the best spots in New Jersey to get up close to the Statue of Liberty and Ellis Island. The park is home to several historic landmarks, including the Central Railroad of New Jersey Terminal (commonly known as Liberty Landing), where immigrants arrived at Ellis Island.

Things to Do: Visit the Liberty Walk, which offers spectacular views of the Statue of Liberty and Manhattan. Explore the Liberty Science Center or take a ferry to Ellis Island and Statue of Liberty for a deeper historical experience.

2. Washington Crossing Historic Park – Washington Crossing
Location: 1112 River Rd, Washington Crossing, PA 18977

Getting There: 1-hour drive from New York City and Philadelphia via Interstate 95.

Overview: This historic site marks the location where General George Washington crossed the Delaware River during the American Revolutionary War in December 1776. The park features monuments, reenactments, and a museum that tells the story of this pivotal moment in American history.

Things to Do: Explore the Washington Crossing Visitor Center, take part in the annual Christmas Crossing reenactment, and visit the nearby Bowman's Hill Wildflower Preserve for hiking and nature walks.

3. Princeton Battlefield State Park – Princeton
Location: 500 Mercer Rd, Princeton, NJ 08540

Getting There: About 1 hour from Philadelphia and 1.5 hours from New York City by car.

Overview: This park commemorates the Battle of Princeton, a pivotal battle during the American Revolutionary War. Visitors can explore the Princeton Battlefield, visit the Clark House, and learn about the battle that marked a significant turning point for the American forces.

Things to Do: Walk the Princeton Battlefield and visit the Clark House to learn more about the battle and its historical significance. Afterward, explore Princeton University's historic campus and visit the Princeton University Art Museum.

4. Batsto Village – Hammonton
Location: 31 Batsto Rd, Hammonton, NJ 08037

Getting There: Located about 1.5 hours from Philadelphia via Route 542.

Overview: A preserved 19th-century village, Batsto Village was once a thriving ironworks community. The village includes original buildings like the Batsto Mansion, General Store, and the Ironmaster's Mansion.

Things to Do: Take a guided tour through the village, learn about early industrial life in New Jersey, and enjoy walking through the nearby Wharton State Forest for a scenic hike or picnic.

DAY TRIPS FROM NEW JERSEY

Exploring New York City (A Short Train Ride Away)

New Jersey's proximity to New York City offers an exciting advantage for travelers. Just a short train ride away, New York City is one of the world's most iconic destinations, boasting countless attractions, vibrant neighborhoods, and world-class dining and entertainment.

Getting There
Train: New Jersey's NJ Transit service connects directly to Penn Station in Manhattan. From Hoboken, Jersey City, or Newark, you can be in New York City in under an hour. For quicker access, take the PATH Train from Jersey City to the World Trade Center or Midtown Manhattan.

Drive: It's just a 1-hour drive from central New Jersey to Manhattan, but be prepared for traffic and costly parking in the city.

Overview
Must-See Attractions:

Statue of Liberty: Take a ferry from Battery Park to see this emblem of freedom up close.

Central Park: A large urban park where you can walk, bike, or enjoy a picnic. There's also boating, ice skating in winter, and a zoo to explore.

The Metropolitan Museum of Art: Explore one of the largest and most prestigious art museums in the world.

Broadway: Watch a world-class theater production on the famous Broadway district.

Times Square: Visit the bustling, neon-lit center of the entertainment world.

Things to Do:

Visit iconic landmarks such as The Empire State Building and One World Trade Center for unbeatable views.

Walk across the Brooklyn Bridge and explore Brooklyn's DUMBO district for stunning views of Manhattan.

Enjoy world-class shopping along Fifth Avenue or in the trendy shops of SoHo.

Visiting Philadelphia, Pennsylvania

Philadelphia, often called the "City of Brotherly Love", is a historic city just a short drive from New Jersey, offering a blend of American history, culture, and vibrant neighborhoods.

Getting There
By Train: From Trenton, Princeton, or Jersey City, you can reach Philadelphia's 30th Street Station in around 1 hour using Amtrak or NJ Transit. It's a quick and comfortable ride with scenic views along the way.

By Car: Drive from New Jersey to Philadelphia in about 1 to 1.5 hours, depending on your starting location. Take Interstate 95 or New Jersey Turnpike.

Overview
Must-See Attractions:

Liberty Bell: A symbol of American independence, located at Independence National Historical Park.

Independence Hall: Where both the Declaration of Independence and the U.S. Constitution were debated and signed.

Philadelphia Museum of Art: Home to the famous Rocky Steps (where Sylvester Stallone ran up in the movie) and an impressive art collection.

Reading Terminal Market: A food lover's paradise, offering everything from Amish specialties to fresh seafood.

Things to Do:

Take a guided tour of Independence Hall and learn about the founding of the U.S.

Explore the Philadelphia Zoo, one of the oldest zoos in the country, home to over 1,300 animals.

Walk along the Schuylkill River Trail or visit the Spruce Street Harbor Park for seasonal outdoor fun.

The Pocono Mountains

The Pocono Mountains, located in northeastern Pennsylvania, are an ideal getaway for outdoor enthusiasts and nature lovers. Known for their picturesque scenery and year-round recreation, the Poconos offer a serene escape from city life.

Getting There
By Car: The Pocono Mountains are a 1.5- to 2-hour drive from New Jersey. Take Interstate 80 or Interstate 476 for a scenic and easy drive to this mountain region.

By Bus: Several bus services, including Martz Trailways, provide direct routes from New Jersey to various towns within the Poconos.

Overview
Must-See Attractions:

Camelback Mountain: A top destination for skiing in winter and water parks during the summer. It also offers zip-lining and mountain biking in warmer months.

Bushkill Falls: Known as the "Niagara of Pennsylvania," these scenic waterfalls offer easy hikes and beautiful views.

Lake Wallenpaupack: A popular spot for boating, fishing, and relaxing by the water.

Things to Do:

Hiking: The Poconos have over 200 miles of hiking trails, including the famous Appalachian Trail, where visitors can explore beautiful woods, cliffs, and mountain views.

Water Sports: Lake Wallenpaupack is great for kayaking, paddleboarding, and swimming.

Winter Sports: In the colder months, the Poconos come alive with ski resorts like Blue Mountain and Camelback, offering snowboarding, skiing, and snow tubing.

Spa and Resorts: Visit one of the Pocono's resort-style hotels for relaxation and pampering, including luxurious spas and wellness retreats.

PRACTICAL TRAVEL TIPS

Safety and Health Tips for Visitors in New Jersey

When traveling in New Jersey, it's important to prioritize your safety and health to ensure a smooth and enjoyable experience. The state offers a diverse range of environments, from bustling cities to quiet nature reserves, and understanding safety tips tailored to each setting can enhance your trip.

General Safety Tips
New Jersey is generally a safe place to visit, but like any destination, it's important to stay aware of your surroundings. In urban areas like Newark, Jersey City, and Atlantic City, always be mindful of your personal belongings, especially in crowded places such as public transport, shopping areas, and popular tourist attractions. Stick to well-lit streets at night, avoid secluded or poorly lit areas, and use trusted rideshare services like Uber or Lyft for safe transportation after dark. For added protection, always lock your car and keep valuables out of sight when parked in public spaces.

Health Tips
When it comes to your health, it's advisable to be prepared for New Jersey's weather, which can vary greatly depending on the season. During summer, temperatures can rise, so stay hydrated and wear sunscreen, especially when visiting outdoor attractions like the Jersey Shore or Liberty State Park. In the winter months, if you plan to visit ski resorts in the Poconos, be sure to dress warmly and take precautions to avoid cold-related illnesses like frostbite. Always check the weather forecast before heading out and pack accordingly, whether it's sunscreen or extra layers for warmth.

Outdoor Activities and Wildlife Safety
For those exploring New Jersey's natural wonders, such as Delaware Water Gap National Recreation Area or the Pocono Mountains, it's crucial to take basic safety precautions. If you plan on hiking or trekking, wear appropriate footwear and bring a first aid kit, water, and a map of the trails. In some areas, you may encounter local wildlife, including deer, bears, and snakes. While wildlife sightings can be exciting, it's important to respect their space and never approach or feed wild animals. Be sure to check with local park rangers or guides for advice on the best practices for safety in natural areas.

Food Safety
New Jersey offers a variety of delicious foods, from pork roll to fresh seafood, but always exercise caution when trying new dishes, especially if you have food allergies or sensitivities. If dining at local markets or food festivals, ensure that food is properly cooked or stored. Stick to reputable restaurants with good hygiene standards. It's also wise to carry hand sanitizer, especially when visiting public areas or outdoor festivals, to reduce the risk of picking up germs.

Travel Insurance and Emergency Contacts
Before heading to New Jersey, consider purchasing travel insurance that covers medical emergencies, lost luggage, and trip cancellations. This can provide peace of mind during your travels. Additionally, familiarize yourself with local emergency numbers. In case of a health emergency, dial 911 for police, fire, or medical services. If you need medical attention during your stay, New Jersey is home to several renowned hospitals, including Hackensack University Medical Center and Morristown Medical Center, where you can receive excellent care.

What to Pack for Your New Jersey Trip

When packing for a trip to New Jersey, it's essential to prepare for the diverse experiences the state offers. From bustling cities like New York City and Jersey City to the outdoor adventures in places like the Pocono Mountains and Jersey Shore, your packing list will depend on the time of year, the activities you plan to do, and the regions you'll visit. Here's a comprehensive guide on what to pack for your New Jersey trip.

Clothing for All Seasons
New Jersey's weather can vary greatly depending on the season, so it's essential to pack versatile clothing that will keep you comfortable throughout your trip.

Spring/Fall: The temperatures can range from mild to chilly, so pack light layers such as long-sleeve shirts, sweaters, and jackets. A lightweight rain jacket is also recommended, as spring and fall bring occasional showers. Comfortable jeans or pants and a pair of sturdy sneakers are great for walking around the cities or exploring outdoor trails.

Summer: Summer in New Jersey can get hot and humid, especially in Jersey Shore or Philadelphia. Pack lightweight, breathable clothing such as T-shirts, shorts, and sundresses. Don't forget a swimsuit for beach trips or water activities, and a hat to protect yourself from the sun. A sunscreen with a high SPF is essential, as UV rays can be strong, especially along the coast.

Winter: Winters in New Jersey can be cold, especially in the Pocono Mountains, where snow is common. Pack warm layers including a winter coat, scarves, gloves, and hats. If you plan to ski or participate in winter sports, be sure to bring thermal wear, snow pants, and waterproof boots.

Footwear
Your footwear depends on the activities you plan to do:

Comfortable walking shoes are a must for city exploration. Whether you're visiting the Statue of Liberty in New York City or strolling through the Philadelphia Museum of Art, a pair of supportive sneakers or comfortable shoes will keep you on your feet all day.

If you're hiking or enjoying nature in places like Delaware Water Gap or High Point State Park, make sure to pack sturdy hiking boots with good traction.

Flip-flops or water shoes are ideal for a day at the beach in Point Pleasant or Long Beach Island.

Weather-Appropriate Accessories

In addition to clothes, it's a good idea to pack a few accessories based on the season:

Sunglasses: Protect your eyes from the sun's glare, especially if you're spending time outdoors at the beach or hiking.

Umbrella: New Jersey can experience sudden rain showers, especially during spring and fall, so pack a small, portable umbrella to stay dry.

Hat: Whether it's for sun protection in the summer or warmth in the winter, hats can be both functional and fashionable.

Health and Hygiene Essentials

While New Jersey has good healthcare facilities, you'll want to have a few health and hygiene items on hand to ensure a smooth trip:

Personal medication: If you're on any medications, be sure to pack enough for the duration of your trip, along with a copy of your prescription just in case.

Hand sanitizer and masks: While COVID-19 restrictions have eased, it's still a good idea to pack hand sanitizer for public spaces and any areas that may require masks.

First aid kit: Pack a small first aid kit with essentials such as band-aids, pain relievers, allergy medicine, and antiseptic wipes, especially if you're spending time outdoors or hiking.

Toiletries: Don't forget essentials like toothbrushes, toothpaste, deodorant, shampoo, conditioner, and any other toiletries you use daily.

Technology and Accessories

In today's digital age, it's important to have the right technology with you for convenience and communication.

Smartphone: For navigation, taking photos, and staying in touch with loved ones.

Portable charger: Keep your phone powered up while on the go, especially if you're using it for directions or taking pictures throughout the day.

Camera: If you enjoy photography, bring a camera to capture the beautiful Jersey Shore, Princeton University, and Pocono Mountains.

Headphones/earbuds: For listening to music or podcasts during long train rides or walks.

Outdoor Gear

If you plan on spending time hiking, skiing, or exploring New Jersey's nature trails, be sure to pack some outdoor-specific gear:

Backpack: For hiking trips or a day at the beach, a lightweight backpack will help you carry your essentials comfortably.

Water bottle: Stay hydrated during hikes or outdoor activities by bringing a reusable water bottle. Many parks and trails in New Jersey have refill stations.

Binoculars: If you're a nature enthusiast, bring a pair of binoculars for bird watching or spotting wildlife in the Poconos or Delaware Water Gap.

Travel Essentials

Ensure you have all the necessary documents and travel items for a smooth trip:

ID and passport: If you're traveling from abroad, don't forget your passport. U.S. residents will need a valid state-issued ID or driver's license for domestic travel.

Travel Insurance: Consider travel insurance for medical emergencies or trip interruptions, especially if you're planning outdoor adventures or international travel.

Tickets and Reservation Confirmations: Always have digital or printed copies of your train, flight, or event tickets, as well as hotel reservations.

Special Considerations

Beach gear: If you're planning to spend a lot of time at the beach, pack items like a towel, beach mat, sunglasses, and a cooler for drinks and snacks. Some beaches, like Point Pleasant and Cape May, have rentals available, but it's always handy to bring your own gear.

Ski gear: If you're heading to the Poconos in winter, check with your resort to see if you need to rent or bring ski equipment like poles, skis, or snowboards.

Useful Phrases and Local Etiquette

When visiting New Jersey, it's important to familiarize yourself with some useful phrases and local etiquette to enhance your experience and interact with locals more comfortably. New Jersey is a culturally diverse state, and its residents come from various backgrounds, which means that politeness, friendliness, and understanding can go a long way. Whether you're exploring Jersey City, hiking in the Poconos, or enjoying the beach in Point Pleasant, here are some phrases and tips to keep in mind.

Useful Phrases
"How you doin'?"
This phrase is commonly associated with New Jersey and is often used as a casual greeting. It's a laid-back, friendly way to ask how someone is doing, much like saying "How's it going?" It's informal and can be used with friends, locals, or people you meet in casual settings.

"What exit?"
This is a New Jersey-specific question, referencing the Garden State Parkway or New Jersey Turnpike, which is used as a way to ask where someone is from. For example, if someone mentions they're from Jersey, you might ask, "What exit?" as a way to learn more about their specific location in the state. It's a fun part of local culture.

"Wawa"
If you hear someone mention "Wawa," don't be confused! It refers to the popular convenience store chain that originated in Pennsylvania but has a strong presence in New Jersey. Wawa is more than just a gas station—it's a beloved place for quick snacks, coffee, and fresh sandwiches. Asking, "Do you want to grab something from Wawa?" is a common question among New Jerseyans.

"Down the shore"
When New Jersey residents refer to heading "down the shore," they're talking about visiting the beaches along the Jersey Shore. If you're planning to hit the coast, this is the phrase you'll hear locals use when discussing their weekend trips or summer vacations.

"Yo" or "Youse"
In casual conversation, some New Jerseyans use "yo" as an informal greeting or interjection. For example, "Yo, what's up?" In certain areas, especially in Northern New Jersey, you might hear "you use" instead of "you" in casual conversation, such as "Youse guys ready for dinner?" It's a fun quirk of the local dialect.

"Jersey" or "Joisey"
Locals often refer to their home state simply as "Jersey," though you may hear a more playful, exaggerated version—"Joisey"—in popular culture or as a friendly local tease. So, when you hear someone say, "I'm from Joisey," you'll know it's a proud Jersey native.

Local Etiquette

Be Respectful of Personal Space
While New Jersey is a densely populated state, especially in cities like Jersey City and Newark, locals generally appreciate their personal space. When riding public transportation or walking through crowded areas like Times Square (if you're visiting NYC) or the Atlantic City Boardwalk, try to respect personal space and be mindful of others. On the beach, it's common for locals to leave a little distance between their group and others to maintain a peaceful atmosphere.

Tipping Etiquette

Tipping is a significant part of the service industry in New Jersey, and it's important to follow the local norms to avoid any misunderstandings. The standard tipping rate for restaurants is typically 15-20% of the bill before tax. For taxis or rideshare drivers like Uber and Lyft, a tip of 10-15% is common. When staying at a hotel, you should tip $1-2 per bag and leave $1-2 per night for housekeeping, especially if the room is thoroughly cleaned. If you're at a bar, it's customary to tip $1-2 per drink or 15-20% of the total bar tab.

Friendly, Direct Communication
New Jerseyans are known for being direct in their communication. They value honesty and appreciate clear, straightforward conversations. If you need help, don't hesitate to ask for directions or information—people are generally happy to assist, though they might give quick and to-the-point answers. That said, always approach others with politeness and a friendly tone.

Driving Etiquette
New Jersey is famous for its aggressive drivers, particularly in cities and busy highways. Be prepared for fast-paced driving, and always make sure to use your turn signals. When driving on the New Jersey Turnpike or Garden State Parkway, you'll notice that the left lane is generally reserved for faster-moving traffic. If you're in the left lane and someone is approaching fast from behind, it's courteous to move over when possible.

Respect for the Beach and Nature
If you're visiting the Jersey Shore or hiking in places like Delaware Water Gap, be sure to respect the natural beauty and cleanliness of the area. Littering is frowned upon, and many beaches and parks in New Jersey have recycling programs, so make sure to dispose of trash properly. In beach towns, local ordinances often enforce rules like no loud music or grilling on public beaches, so always check signs and follow guidelines to ensure a positive experience for everyone.

Punctuality
In New Jersey, being punctual is considered a sign of respect, especially in professional settings. If you're meeting someone for a business meeting or formal event, it's best to arrive on time or even a little early.

That said, if you're meeting friends for a casual outing or a meal, there's usually a little more flexibility, but arriving more than 15 minutes late might be considered rude.

Respecting Regional Differences
New Jersey has a diverse population, with strong influences from Italian, Polish, African-American, and other communities. You'll find neighborhoods and towns that celebrate different cultures and traditions. When visiting areas with a strong cultural identity, be respectful of local customs and traditions. In many cases, locals take great pride in their heritage and appreciate others taking an interest in their backgrounds.

USEFUL RESOURCES

Tourism Websites & Apps for New Jersey

For a smooth and enjoyable trip to New Jersey, there are several tourism websites and apps that can help you find the best activities, events, dining options, and more. These resources offer up-to-date information on attractions, accommodations, and local happenings.

1. Visit New Jersey – Official Tourism Website
Website: www.visitnj.org

Overview: The official tourism website of New Jersey is your go-to resource for comprehensive information on attractions, events, dining, and accommodations. Whether you're visiting the Jersey Shore, exploring Princeton University, or hiking in the Poconos, you'll find detailed guides, itineraries, and travel tips to make your trip easier.

Features: Interactive maps, event calendars, suggested itineraries, and seasonal guides for outdoor activities.

2. NJ Transit App
Website: www.njtransit.com

Overview: The NJ Transit app is essential for getting around New Jersey. It offers real-time train, bus, and light rail schedules, route information, and mobile ticketing for a smooth travel experience in the state.

Features: Plan your trip, buy tickets, check real-time transit updates, and view alerts on delays or service changes. It's a great tool for navigating New Jersey's public transport system.

3. Yelp
Website: www.yelp.com

Overview: Yelp is a popular app for discovering the best restaurants, bars, and attractions in New Jersey. It provides user reviews, ratings, and photos, helping you make informed decisions on where to eat, shop, or explore.

Features: Search for highly rated places by category, read reviews, see photos, and even make reservations or order takeout through the app.

4. TripAdvisor
Website: www.tripadvisor.com

Overview: TripAdvisor provides detailed reviews of hotels, restaurants, activities, and attractions. You can use it to plan your itinerary, find recommendations based on your interests, and read advice from fellow travelers.

Features: Access reviews, itineraries, and travel forums, and book hotels and activities directly through the app.

Emergency Contacts & Services in New Jersey

It's always good to know where to turn in case of an emergency while traveling. Whether you're visiting New Jersey's cities or its natural reserves, the following services and contacts are important for ensuring your safety.

1. Emergency Services
Emergency Number: Dial 911 for police, fire, and medical emergencies throughout New Jersey.

Local Police: Each town or city has its local police department. For example:

Newark Police Department: (973) 733-6000

Jersey City Police Department: (201) 547-5477

Atlantic City Police Department: (609) 347-5780

2. Hospitals & Medical Care
New Jersey is home to several reputable hospitals and urgent care centers across the state. Some major medical centers include:

Hackensack University Medical Center – Hackensack, NJ
Phone: (551) 996-2000

Morristown Medical Center – Morristown, NJ
Phone: (973) 971-5000

RWJ University Hospital – New Brunswick, NJ
Phone: (732) 828-3000

Cape Regional Health System – Cape May Court House, NJ
Phone: (609) 463-2000

For minor health concerns or injuries, New Jersey also has numerous urgent care centers available in major cities and towns.

3. Non-Emergency Services
NJ Poison Control Center: (1-800-222-1222)
For non-emergency poison-related incidents or inquiries, this number is staffed with medical professionals.

State Health Hotline: (1-800-962-1253)
For health-related questions or assistance, including mental health, substance abuse, and other general health inquiries.

4. Local Fire Departments
New Jersey Division of Fire Safety: (609) 633-6130

Jersey City Fire Department: (201) 547-4545

Atlantic City Fire Department: (609) 347-5570

For general fire-related emergencies or information about fire safety and prevention, these departments can provide the necessary support.

Language & Translation Help in New Jersey

New Jersey is a linguistically diverse state with many residents speaking languages other than English. While English is the primary language, you'll encounter many Spanish, Portuguese, and other language speakers. Here are some resources to help with language barriers.

1. Language Translation Apps
Google Translate: This popular app supports over 100 languages and can instantly translate text, images (via camera), and even speech. It's a great tool for overcoming language barriers in both urban and rural areas.

iTranslate: This app also offers voice translation and offline capabilities, perfect for travel in areas where Wi-Fi might be unavailable.

SayHi: A simple-to-use app for voice translation, great for conversations in real-time.

2. Spanish-Speaking Communities

Spanish is one of the most widely spoken languages in New Jersey, especially in cities like Jersey City, Newark, and Paterson. Many signs, menus, and even public services are available in both English and Spanish. You can expect Spanish-speaking staff in most larger stores, hotels, and tourist attractions.

3. Multilingual Services

NJ 211: A free service that offers assistance in multiple languages, including Spanish, Portuguese, and more. Dial 211 for help with social services, health resources, and general information.

Local Libraries: Many public libraries in New Jersey offer translation services or language support. The Newark Public Library and the Jersey City Free Public Library are examples where non-English speaking visitors can find resources and help.

4. Professional Translators

For important documents, medical needs, or official meetings, consider hiring a professional translator. New Jersey has a number of language service providers who can assist with legal documents, medical translation, and business-related services.

FINAL TIPS FOR FIRST-TIME VISITORS

Local Customs and Etiquette in New Jersey

New Jersey is known for its diversity, with residents hailing from a variety of cultural and ethnic backgrounds. While the state's urban and suburban areas offer a fast-paced, cosmopolitan feel, the people of New Jersey are generally friendly and direct in their communication. Understanding the local customs and etiquette will help ensure you have a positive and respectful experience.

Politeness and Directness
New Jerseyans are known for their straightforwardness. When interacting with locals, be prepared for direct communication. This isn't considered rude but rather a reflection of the state's no-nonsense approach to conversation. People here value honesty, so don't be surprised if someone offers their opinion without much hesitation.

At the same time, respectful politeness is important. When in social or formal settings, be sure to say "please," "thank you," and "excuse me." Small gestures of courtesy, such as holding the door open for someone or offering a friendly greeting, are greatly appreciated.

Driving Etiquette
Driving in New Jersey can be intense, especially in busy urban areas or during rush hour. Locals are known for driving fast and can sometimes seem aggressive on the road. If you're not used to this pace, it might be a bit overwhelming. However, it's essential to use turn signals, follow the speed limits, and be aware of local driving laws.

If you're driving on the Garden State Parkway or New Jersey Turnpike, stay in the right lane unless you're overtaking another vehicle. The left lane is often reserved for faster drivers, so be mindful of traffic etiquette.

Tipping Etiquette
Tipping is a significant part of the service industry in New Jersey, and it's customary to leave a tip of 15-20% at restaurants. For taxis and rideshares (like Uber and Lyft), a 10-15% tip is common. For hotel staff, a $1-2 per night for housekeeping and $1-2 per bag for bellhops is appreciated. If you're getting drinks at a bar, tipping $1-2 per drink is the standard.

Beaches and Public Spaces
New Jersey's beaches, such as those along the Jersey Shore, often have specific rules and customs. For example, no loud music or drinking alcohol on the beach, and it's important to clean up after yourself. Many beach towns have ordinances in place to maintain cleanliness and ensure a good experience for all visitors.

When visiting public spaces or parks, make sure to dispose of your trash properly, use designated areas for grilling, and be respectful of others around you. Noise levels are generally kept low in public parks, so be mindful of keeping your conversations or music at a respectful volume.

Best Photo Ops in New Jersey

New Jersey offers numerous scenic spots and iconic landmarks that are perfect for photography, whether you're a professional photographer or simply someone looking to capture memories. From stunning city views to breathtaking natural landscapes, here are some of the best spots for taking photos.

1. Liberty State Park – Jersey City
Location: Liberty Landing Marina, Jersey City, NJ 07305

Best For: Views of Statue of Liberty and Manhattan skyline.

Why It's a Great Photo Op: The Liberty State Park offers incredible views of the Statue of Liberty, Ellis Island, and the New York Harbor. You can also get beautiful shots of the Manhattan skyline from here, making it an ideal location for both daytime and sunset photos.

Tip: Capture the Statue of Liberty with the New Jersey waterfront in the foreground for a unique angle.

2. Asbury Park Boardwalk – Asbury Park
Location: Asbury Park, NJ 07712

Best For: Beach, boardwalk, and vintage charm.

Why It's a Great Photo Op: Asbury Park is a perfect blend of beach vibes and quirky charm. The boardwalk is lined with art galleries, funky shops, and vintage architecture, making it a vibrant spot for photos. Sunsets over the beach are also stunning.

Tip: Snap a picture near the iconic Asbury Park Carousel, which adds a nostalgic touch to your photos.

3. High Point State Park – Sussex
Location: 1480 State Rt. 23, Sussex, NJ 07461

Best For: Mountain views and panoramic landscapes.

Why It's a Great Photo Op: As the highest point in New Jersey, High Point State Park offers panoramic views that stretch into Pennsylvania and New York. From the High Point Monument, you can take in expansive views of the Pocono Mountains, Appalachian Mountains, and beyond.

Tip: Visit early in the morning or around sunset for dramatic lighting and vibrant skies.

4. Princeton University Campus – Princeton
Location: Princeton, NJ 08544

Best For: Historic architecture and Ivy League beauty.

Why It's a Great Photo Op: The Princeton University campus is one of the most beautiful college campuses in the country. With its historic Gothic buildings, well-maintained lawns, and the iconic University Chapel, it offers numerous picturesque settings.

Tip: Take photos of the University Chapel and Nassau Hall. The university's gardens are also great for serene, nature-filled shots.

5. The Delaware Water Gap – Warren County
Location: Warren County, NJ 07827

Best For: Nature, waterfalls, and river views.

Why It's a Great Photo Op: The Delaware Water Gap offers a stunning landscape with lush forests, towering cliffs, and the Delaware River. The area is home to several waterfalls, including the breathtaking Buttermilk Falls.

Tip: Hike the Dunnfield Creek Trail for a chance to capture the falls in all their glory.

How to Enjoy New Jersey Like a Local
To truly experience New Jersey like a local, it's essential to step off the beaten path and embrace the state's hidden gems, quirky traditions, and vibrant neighborhoods. Here are some tips to help you enjoy New Jersey like a true Garden State native.

1. Head "Down the Shore"
When locals say they're going "down the shore," they're referring to visiting the Jersey Shore, a beloved summer destination with a variety of beach towns. Each town has its own unique vibe: Asbury Park is known for its artsy, hip atmosphere, while Wildwood offers a classic boardwalk experience with amusement rides and arcades. Try renting bikes, taking in the beach vibes, or stopping by a local seafood shack for the freshest catch.

2. Take a Ride on a Local Diner
New Jersey is famous for its diners, which are open 24/7 and serve up hearty American fare, from breakfast classics to comfort food. Belmar Diner and Max's Deli in Hoboken are iconic spots where you can enjoy a pork roll sandwich or classic New Jersey cheesesteak.

Tip: Don't forget to try Taylor Ham (also called pork roll), a staple of New Jersey breakfast menus.

3. Experience the Local Arts Scene
New Jersey has a thriving arts scene that's often overlooked. Head to Montclair for art galleries, Asbury Park for live music, or Red Bank for theater at the Count Basie Center for the Arts. Whether you enjoy indie films, theater performances, or jazz music, New Jersey offers a rich cultural experience.

Tip: Keep an eye on local event listings for festivals, art walks, and music events that celebrate New Jersey's artistic side.

4. Explore New Jersey's Small Towns
While New Jersey's big cities are exciting, some of the most charming experiences can be found in smaller towns like Princeton, Cape May, and Morristown. These towns are rich in history, with well-preserved architecture, charming streets, and unique boutique shops.

Tip: Explore Cape May's Victorian district or stroll along the tree-lined streets of Princeton, stopping for coffee at one of the many local cafes.

Printed in Dunstable, United Kingdom

71232684R00054